Preserving the Past

THE PAST

SALEM MORAVIANS' RECEIPTS & RITUALS

A Little Salem™ Book
First in a Series

Carolina Avenue Press

BOONVILLE, NC

This book's highest purpose is to reproduce authentic archival materials. All recipes are reproduced as they are found within the originals. All remedies are included strictly for preservation purposes and not for medical application; the archives and publisher are not engaging in rendering medical service and the information herein is not intended to replace the services of trained health professionals or be a substitute for medical advice. The archives and publisher specifically disclaim any such liability. This book is intended for historical documentation and recreational cooking.

Preserving the Past: Salem Moravians' Receipts & Rituals

published by

114 Carolina Avenue South, P.O. Box 775, Boonville, NC 27011
www.carolinapress.com

First edition 2003.
Second printing 2006.

ISBN-10: 0-9718231-3-8
ISBN-13: 978-0-9718231-3-6

Printed in Canada

DESIGN BY Whitline Ink Incorporated
www.whitlineink.com   (336)367-6914

DESIGN NOTES: *The skeleton of the cover originated from a book published in 1854, which belonged to Emily-Sarah Lineback's great-great grandfather John Anderson Fishel, a devoted Moravian, husband to Emeline Leonard, and father to David, Mary, and America (Adelia). Cover inset drawing of Moravian lovefeast ©2003, 2006 K. Scott Whitaker.*

dedicated in memory of our Moravian ancestors and
in honor of those who are carrying on the traditions...

YOU ARE HELPING PRESERVE HISTORY

THE MORAVIAN ARCHIVES is one of the oldest archives in the country, predating national institutions. This book is its first published collection of recipes and helps mark the celebration of its 250th anniversary. Your purchase of *Preserving the Past* is helping the archives—a portion of the proceeds from each book sold is donated back to the archives so that its work and preservation may continue.

ABOUT THE MORAVIAN ARCHIVES

THE MORAVIAN ARCHIVES began with the diaries of the first settlers of the Wachovia tract in 1753. It preserves continuous records from that date, with over one million pages of diaries, minutes, church registers, ledgers, maps, and other materials. The archives preserves the records which have formed the basis of the restoration and interpretive programs of Old Salem and Historic Bethabara Park. It continues to add to the collections by receiving records from Moravian churches of the Southern Province.

For more information about the archives or to become a Friend of the Archives, write to Box L, Winston-Salem, NC 27108, search *www.moravianarchives.org,* or simply visit the Archie K. Davis Center situated within Old Salem.

"We hold arrival Lovefeast here,
In Carolina land,
A company of Brethren true,
A little Pilgrim Band,
Called by the Lord to be of those
Who through the whole world go,
To bear Him witness everywhere,
And naught but Jesus know."

—*verse sung upon reaching the Wachovia tract in North
Carolina after traveling from Bethlehem, Pennsylvania*[1]

Our ancestors used paper judiciously. If a book's original content became less than useful, they would paste new writings and clippings to it. One of many examples is where the Salem family of Van Vlecks used the backside of the cover of *The Family Receipt Book & Useful Medical Adviser 1852* to write and paste receipts.

TABLE OF CONTENTS

"When the land has been settled it will be said that it is a fruitful land, but the Brethren have been the first to cultivate it...Therefore all that can be said is that it is land on which everything grows that is planted."[2]

PREFACE

BOOKS ABOUND on the settlement of Salem and its Moravian inhabitants. One reason we know so much about these early North Carolina settlers is because Moravians always have been meticulous recordkeepers; there are over one million examples housed in the Moravian Archives. (Located within Old Salem and dating its beginning at 1753, it is one of the oldest archives in the United States.)

Both genders of Moravians took notekeeping seriously. Women kept and continually added to their handmade "receipt books," which often evolved into a compendium of traditional recipes that also included cleaning tips, etiquette rules, and other information regarded as useful. These items converged into an inclusive record of home and community.

Preserving the Past: Salem Moravians' Receipts & Rituals showcases an authentic and edible part of this settlement's history. Recipes are a time machine into the heritage of a place and people, showing what grew in and around the area, what items were accessible, and what dishes were usual. As someone said, recipes put flesh on the bare bones of an era. Moravian cooking has its roots in Germany with some Pennsylvania Dutch adaptations; no doubt, cooks again adapted and copied some of North Carolina's (English-inspired) dishes.

By paralleling recipes from centuries ago to dishes of today, you can compare and contrast the availability of ingredients as well as how typical tastes vary. It's important to note that in the 1700s and 1800s, it took several years for certain spices to reach Salem; thus, the flavors were different (often muted) in contrast to fresh spices that are available in markets today. Baking powder didn't yet exist in its current form. (Search the glossary to find its forerunner along with other uncommon words you'll encounter.) Refer to the tables section for necessary conversion charts.

Brackets [ ] indicate where a word is undecipherable, unclear, or where a word has been added for clarity. Be aware that words and sentences were left as they were found—some with variant or quaint (mis)spellings (even an occasional word misspelled multiple different ways), a few grammatical issues, or inconsistencies among the different recipe collections (for instance, "lb" versus "lb." versus "pound")—these were left to be true to the authors' renderings and the time period.

The main challenge of many of the recipes is the absence of the all-important directions; indeed, our foremothers likely felt that if they wrote down the essential parts, certainly each generation after (as information and methods were passed down) would know the basics of what to do. Fast forward two centuries, and ingredients and usual ways of preparing food are drastically different. Some of their original intentions are not easily known or inferred.

Keep in mind, too, that terminology in some of the recipes differs from current usage. For instance, "cake" could also mean cookie or bread; "gravy" often referred to stock; many of their puddings were bagged and boiled, resulting in a different consistency from modern versions.

These receipts are authentic and unaltered from the state in which they have been preserved. You may find, as some present-day Moravians did during some of the taste tests, that you want to alter the recipe to make it more pleasing to twenty-first-century palettes. You may also delight in some of the recipes' old-fashioned characteristics. The paramount concern in compiling this collection was its historic authenticity, but in your kitchen please do as you wish to make the dish yours. These recipes were passed down from earlier beginnings and quite assuredly modified at times before (and after) being captured by the pen. Cooks have always tweaked recipes to make them uniquely theirs, and no less is expected of you.

This book holds the framework of Moravian rituals and through faith and food shows glimpses into the lives of those behind the honored events that have been sustained throughout the centuries.

Moravians enjoy a past steeped in devout tradition, and the denomination is preserved by a love just as vibrant. Both love and tradition were passed from one generation to the next in the simple but essential observance of sharing meals together, not only as a family but also as a congregation.

Turn these pages to discover and delight in the Moravians' foundation of faith, family, and food.

INTRODUCTION

A BRIEF BACKGROUND ON THE MORAVIANS

ORIGINATING IN Bohemia, the Moravians' beginning dates back to John Hus, whose preachings earned him a martyr's death in 1415. His most devout followers formed the Unitas Fratrum (Unity of Brethren), which flourished throughout Bohemia and neighboring Moravia until the Thirty Years War (1618–1648) destroyed the church, forcing its members into hiding or exile. In the early 1700s, a small band of members secretly fled Moravia to what is now part of Germany, to the estate of Count Von Zinzendorf; a deeply religious man, he allowed them to establish the village of Herrnhut ("the Lord's Watch") on his land.

A combination of mission and management (and the Count's help) led them to other countries, including North America. Their towns' successes drew the attention of Lord Granville in North Carolina, who invited them to help settle the Carolina wilderness. In 1753, the Moravians purchased nearly 100,000 acres, which they called Wachovia. A congregation settlement was first established in Bethabara (1753), then Bethania (1756), and in 1766, the central, commercial town of Salem (*shalom*—"peace"). Its townspeople approached their dwelling place as they did their souls—always to be guarded, improved, and celebrated.

One distinction of original Moravian settlements is that each citizen had to be a church member, and church elders were involved in all aspects of inhabitants' lives. Each individual was expected to contribute to bettering the quality of life for the community by using his or her God-given talents. This cooperative atmosphere sparked an entrepreneurial spirit (but tempered competition) and fostered artisans. Above all, the emphasis of the Moravian "Brothers" and "Sisters" of Salem rested on their faith; their focus was upon the church, the family, and work.

The Salem Moravians haven't merely secured a place within archives, books, and Old Salem reenactments; their commitment continues worldwide within present-day Moravians: *"in essentials, unity; in nonessentials, liberty; in all things, love."*

There are five main recipe collections housed at the Moravian Archives, each representing a Salem family. The Van Vleck collection (VVC) is the largest. The other four are Vogler (VC); Crist (CC), Winkler (WC), and an unnamed (UC) collection. Each is duly noted.

1

HELPFUL HOUSEHOLD RECEIPTS

WHETHER MARRIED or single, Salem women were industrious. Moreover, their work contributed greatly toward the town's success, economically and socially.

The Single Sisters ran a girls school, a laundry, and grew vegetables both for their own use and for sale. Married Sisters completed the gamut of daily chores—cooking, housekeeping tasks, childcare; other chores were weekly, such as washing and ironing clothes. Some tasks were seasonal: gardens were planted in the spring; summer was filled with tending them; fall brought with it the harvest, drying and preserving meat, and "putting up" food for the winter.

Running a household has always been a full-time job. Certainly, this is one reason why the Sisters collected the following items, preserving them within their homemade receipt books. Just like we do today, they were always on the watch for helpful tips and timesavers to make their workload lighter.

To Polish Stoves

Make a weak alum water and mix your British lustre with it, say 2 teaspoonfulls to a gill of alum water. Let the stove be cold; brush it with the mixture, then take a dry brush and dry lustre and rub the stove till it is perfectly dry. Should any part become so dry before polishing as to look gray, moisten with the wet brush and proceed as above. I sometimes take tolerable strong alum water and go over the stove one morning and polish it the next. (CC)

* * * * *

Bake ovens in Salem were closely inspected and regulated—how they were built, what surrounded them, how they were maintained— because the threat of fire was always high.

To Mend Cracked Stoves

Cracks in stoves and stove pipes are readily closed by a paste made of ashes and salt with water. Iron turnings or filings, sal ammoniac, and water make a harder and more durable cement. (VVC)

To Mend Iron Pots

To repair cracks, etc., in iron pots or pans, mix some finely sifted lime with well-beaten whites of eggs, till reduced to a paste; then add some iron file dust, apply the composition to the injured part, and it will soon become hard and fit for use. (VVC)

To Mend Broken China

Take unslaked lime, made fine by pounding or grinding, [then] mix with the white of an egg to the consistency of starch or paint; thoroughly cleanse and dry the edges to be united, then apply the mixture to the parts to be cemented, place them together firmly, and let them become perfectly dry. Articles thus mended can be handled or washed without injury. (VVC)

Cracked Tea-Kettle

An old cracked tea-kettle is one of the most useful articles in the pot closet. When you have a cracked tea-kettle, then you have the best thing in the world for cooking potatoes. Wash them, cut off the end where the eyes are thick, and then put them in the tea-kettle without any water, and hang it over a moderate fire, and in half an hour or so, you will have your potatoes baked, dried, and mealy—and just the very thing for a good dinner. The noise of the kettle allows all the moisture of the vegetables to escape, and a cracked tea-kettle is essential to good eating. (VVC)

How to Clear a Glass

Rub the glass chrystal with a piece of lead; that will make it clear and bright. (VVC)

To Prevent the Smoking of a Lamp

Soak the wick in strong vinegar, and dry thoroughly before using. (VVC)

A Wash to Clean Oil Pictures

Make a lye with clean water and wood ashes; in this dip a sponge, rub the picture over, and it will clean it perfectly. (VVC)

Washing Preparation

Of all the preparations I have used, and they have been numerous, I give the preference to the following: Put one pound of saltpetre into a gallon of water, and keep it in a corked jug, two tablespoonfuls for a pint of soap; soak, wash, and boil as usual. This bleaches the clothes beautifully without injuring the fabric. It is particularly valuable for removing grass stains from the knees of the little boys' pantaloons. (VVC)

To Remove Fruit Stains from Linen

Rub the part on each side with Yellow Soap, then tie up a piece of Pearl Ash in the cloth; soak well in hot water or boil; afterward, expose the stained part to the sun and air till removed. (VVC)

Waterproofing for Boots and Shoes

One pint Linseed Oil, one-fourth pint Turpentine, one-fourth pound Yellow Wax, one-fourth pound Burgundy Pitch—melt together with a gentle heat. Warm when required for use, and rub into the leather before a hot fire. (VVC)

To Prevent Flies from Sitting or Laying Their Dung Anywhere

Take a large bunch of leeks, soak them for 5 or 6 days in a pail full of water, and wash your picture or any other piece of furniture with it. The flies will never come near anything so washed. (VVC)

To Revive a Fading Flower

Cut the stalk and hold it a few moments in the flame of the candle, and then set the flower again in the cold water, when it will recover its strength almost visibly after this violent assistance, and blossom immediately. So they say. (VVC)

Excellent Hair Wash

1 oz borax, 1/2 oz camphor, powder. These ingredients very fine. (UC)

Soft Soap for the Ladies

Take a pound of castile soap, scrape it into small pieces and put it in the fire with a little water. Stir it till it becomes a smooth paste, pour into a bowl and when cold, add some lavender or essence of any kind, beat with a [spoon]. When well mixed, thicken... (VVC)

Durable Ink

A little lunar caustic, fill up with vinegar, and cork tightly. Prepare the larger bottle by putting in a teaspoonful of salt of tartar and a lump of gum arabic the size of a hickory nut, then fill up with rain water. Cork both bottles tightly and set them for two days in the sun. The weather must be clear when you mark: wet with the mixture and dry in the sun a day. (VVC)

Grafting Wax
"best"

1 lb of Rosin, 1/4 lb beeswax, and 1/4 lb of [beef] tallow. Melt them in a skillet and mix well. It should remain in the vessel and be used warm as needed. Applying warm does no injury to the graft; it will not crack in cool or dry weather or run in warm. (CC)

Cement for Grafting
"good"

1 oz pitch (or Burgundy pitch and no turpentine)
1 oz Rosin
1/2 [oz] of beeswax
1/4 [oz] of hogs lard
1/4 oz turpentine
to be boiled up together but not to be used till you can bear your finger in it. (CC)

Cement for Jars & Bottles

Take one third beeswax, 2/3 rosin. Pound the rosin very fine, put it with beeswax in some suitable vessel, and set over the fire to melt. When quite melted, take it off the fire and stir in some brick dust, till the mixture becomes as thick as melted sealing wax. Then plaster it warm round the cover of your preserve or pickle jars. If you use it for bottles, first cork them tight, then dip the tops into the cement. (CC)

Salem sported an elaborate, modern water system. Wooden pipes connected to surrounding higher-elevation springs provided water to several cisterns within the village, utilizing gravity. Townspeople drew and carried water from the cisterns.

* * * * *

Liquid Glue

"Will glue wood or anything." Dated Oct. 1, 1883.

Dissolve glue in strong vinegar, [let get] very hot over the fire then add about 1/4 [teaspoon] of alcohol and a little alum. Will keep for years in a stopped bottle. (VVC)

To Purify River or Any Other Muddy Water

Dissolve half an ounce of alum in a pint of warm water, and stirring it about in a puncheon of water just taken from any river, all the impurities will soon settle to the bottom, and in a day or two it will become as clear as the finest spring water. (VVC)

Milk in Thunderstorms

From a newspaper clipping glued within the receipt book.

We have heard great complaints from dairy women about their milk getting sour during a thunderstorm, although perfectly sweet a short time previous. The following plans will in a great degree prevent this: All the pans containing milk ought to be placed upon a non-conductor of electricity, such as blocks of baked wood, pieces of glass, or wood that has been well painted or varnished. These are articles most easily provided. Beeswax, feathers, and woolen cloth are also non-conductors, but inconvenient to be used. All these articles will insulate the pan and prevent the electric fluid from entering, which is the cause of acidity, or is in fact the principle of acidity itself. (VVC)

* * * * *

Although Salem Moravians had their own chickens and pigs, at first they were not permitted to keep cows. Originally, milk was provided by dairy farmers who had made arrangements to supply the town.

Paper Lighter with Curled Ends

The Body of the Lighter: Cut a piece of white paper, nearly one inch in width and 10 inches long. Roll this paper spirally round 3 or 4 rushes joined together and paste the top of the lighter. When it is made it ought to be 6 1/3 inches long. (VVC)

Ornaments for the Lighter

The orn[aments] consist of 6 branches, the paper being curled and falling like a weeping willow. To make a branch, do a [fold]. Cut a piece of flower paper of any color you like, 8 2/3 inches long and 2 inches wide. Cut with scissors a fringe 1 1/3 inch in depth; there then remains 2/3 of an inch of plain paper. The fringe is not very fine; you must give it about 12 cuts in each inch. When it is thus fringed all around, curl it by rolling 4 or 5 of the cut pieces between the scissors and your thumb. Then turn the paper spirally on a knitting needle not very thick. Do 5 more the same way. Join them together, so as to form a branch by the air of a little paste, then paste them to the thickest end of the lighter. 4 lighters of this kind make a very pretty [ ], each one is made of a different color. The body is of rather strong white paper. (VVC)

Ornaments for Candlesticks

Cut a band of green cardboard two thirds of an inch high and about 2 1/2 inches long, make it into a round and [glue] it strongly. The round must be large enough for a wax candle to [stand]. When the [glue] is quite dry, make 12 cuts at equal distances, care being taken not to cut it too near the other edge, as about 1/6 of an inch must remain [uncut] to surround the candles. Then open the twelve pieces of cardboard with a pair of scissors in the same manner that children arrange the straws for soap bubbles. On the cardboard thus prepared, the ornament is made in the following manner.

FIRST round is composed of a piece of paper of a pretty green, prepared for flowers, 1 1/3 inches high and 16 inches long. With very fine pointed scissors cut it on one side into a fine fringe, resembling that of a bonbon cracker, but only 1/3 inch deep. Take the cardboard in the left hand, and the green paper in the right and with a brush and some paste, fix it inside the cardboard, folding the paper as you paste it to the divisions of the card; you will have to make about two folds in each division to use the 16 inches in the round.

SECOND round consists of a piece of paper of whatever color is preferred. This piece is 2/3 of an inch longer than the first and 1/6 of an inch higher. It is cut in the same manner as the green one and pasted inside the cardboard on the green, and folded in the same manner.

THIRD round. A piece of paper 17 1/3 inches long, 1 2/3 high, fringe and paste inside as described above. Paste them one a little above the other that the ornament may be nicely rounded. The fringe of the first round comes above the cardboard; the fringe of the other rounds forms a kind of fine mop which is very pretty.

This little work is very amusing and very cheap. The colors may be varied according to taste; the 1st round must, however, always be in green paper. (VVC)

The Diary of the Congregation in Salem
Dec. 24, 1780

"First there was the Christmas lovefeast for the children… and at the close of a written Christmas verse a lighted candle was given to each child, and they carried the lighted candles to their homes. The weather was calm and pleasant. Later the adult members had a lovefeast."[3]

Whitening Beeswax

My way…is to make the wax and pour it while hot into a quantity of the coldest water I can get; the cold water sets it quickly and it will look like a large sponge; then take out of the water and lay it in a sunny place out of doors, leaving it there until white enough to suit, occasionally turning it over. It bleaches in a short time. Then melt again and mold it into any desired shape. Sometimes I strain it through a cloth at the final melting. (VVC)

Candles

Dated April 1885.

To purify Tallow: Throw in powdered "quick lime" (as much as you think proper). Dip the wicks in lime water and saltpetre on making. To 1 gallon of water, add 2 ounces of saltpetre and 1/2 [ ] of lime. It improves the light and prevents the tallow from burning [improperly]. (VVC)

THE CHRISTMAS LOVEFEAST CANDLE

AT THE END OF THE Christmas Eve Lovefeast and Candle Service, each participant is given a candle made of beeswax and tallow. Beeswax is used because it's one of the purer waxes. Around the bottom of the candle is a red paper frill. Tradition says that the beeswax and tallow represent Christ's purity, the lighted wick, divinity, and the red frill, atonement (some say Christ's blood sacrifice); in modern times, the candle serves as a reminder that Christ declared, "I am the Light of the world" (John 8:12, John 9:5), and likewise "Ye are the light of the world…" (Matthew 5:14). After everyone's candle is lighted, while singing the last hymn's final stanza, worshipers hold their candles high toward heaven, symbolizing a rededication of their lives to Jesus. Until the end of the nineteenth century, only children received candles; afterward, you could see them moving down the streets toward their homes, each carefully holding a lighted candle. Those who lived close and could keep their flame intact until reaching home would then use it to light the candles on the Christmas tree.

A FEW NOTES ON ETIQUETTE

JUST BECAUSE SALEM was a small community didn't mean the ladies and gentlemen living within weren't aware of nor concerned with etiquette. The following two clippings were carefully preserved within one of the Van Vleck receipt books.

Notes and Cards of Invitations

* Invitations should be sent in the name of the lady of the home. The usual form is simple "Mrs. _____ requests the pleasure of Mr. and Mrs. _____'s company on _____ _____." Replies or invitations couched in unusual forms of speech (unless the part is a very small and sociable one) denote a want of breeding.

* A note of invitation or reply is always enclosed in an envelope.

* Sealing wax should be of fancy colors, or if a wafer is used, it must be a transparent one, designed for ladies' notes.

* For invitations use finely glazed and gild edged paper, perfectly unadorned unless with the stamp of your crest or initials. (VVC)

Bowing and Other Salutations

* It is bad taste to curtsey in the street, and is equally bad taste to bow stiffly. A slight bend of the body, at the same time that you incline the head, forms the most graceful and affable salutation.

* A smile is a natural greeting on meeting a friend, and if it is necessary to bow coldly to an acquaintance, it is quite as well not to bow at all.

* A gentleman should always lift his hat entirely from his head on saluting a lady—unless he does this, his salutation deserves no return.

* Bows should be mutual and made at the same moment, but when they are unavoidably otherwise, the lady should bow first to the gentleman as a token that she permits him to recognize her. If she does not do so, he is not at liberty to salute her, and runs the risk of finding his salutation unanswered.

* Low curtsies are now entirely obsolete, unless you are curtsying to a very old lady—then, as a mark of respect, you may bend lower than usual.

* When a lady is introduced to you, you may say, "I am very happy to make your acquaintance," but there are a few cases where this remark can be addressed with propriety to a gentleman from a lady. It is always a favor for him to be presented to her, therefore, the pleasure should be on his side.

* "I am happy to see you," is a very usual expression on greeting a visitor. (VVC)

2

MEDICINAL REMEDIES

T HE SALEM MORAVIANS, as did other people of the day, used herbs for seasoning food and also for medicinal purposes. Then it was strongly believed and practiced that for every ailment and disease there was a natural substance that could prevent, cure, or ease it. Almost every household kept an herb garden, and cooks always kept an ample supply and variety of herbs and spices in their cupboards. Ginger was one popular choice because in a powdered form it could aid baking, and in candied chunks it served as first aid (a piece laid on an aching tooth helped ease the pain; ginger tea helped one's stomach).

They made preventive tonics that were taken for any number of reasons including to thin the blood and ward off laziness. Sassafras root tea was one of many possible concoctions.

For an Internal Bruise or Soreness

Make a strong tea of life everlasting and drink of it freely. (UC)

* * * * *

Also known as "sweet everlasting," life everlasting is a herbaceous biennial with green leaves and clusters of small, white flower heads. Its usual height is from 1–3 feet. Through the early 1900s, it was one of the most highly regarded remedies for sale in local markets of the Southern United States. It was typically used in several ways: as an astringent tea, a bitter herbal cold medicine, and the leaves and blossoms chewed. [4]

* * * * *

For Sore Throat

Grease the throat outside with rabbit grease and drink tea of life everlasting; gargle with vinegar, salt, and pepper, also use alum and honey mixed. (UC)

Cure for Cough

1/2 a teaspoonful of pulverized alum in a little molasses. (UC)

Cough Syrup Recipe

Put 1 quart horehound for 1 quart water and boil down to a pint.
Add 2 or 3 sticks of licorice and add a tablespoonful of essence
of lemon. A tablespoonful 3 times or more a day. (VVC)

Cure for Dysentery or Flux

Take 2 tablespoonsful of vinegar, 1 teaspoonful of black pepper,
1 teaspoon full of salt, mix and drink. (UC)

* * * * *

*Many wild plants grew in Salem, including calves foot (Adron),
which was said to be good for asthmas and lung trouble...Angelica,
a possible antidote for poison; Andrew Cross (a snakeroot), a small
dark green plant with leaves forming a cross, which was most effi-
cacious when boiled in milk and drunk or applied externally; and
Allermanns Harnisch, which was like a large nettle and used in
curing wounds.* [5]

* * * * *

For Consumption

1 quart of vinegar, 4 pods of red pepper, boiled down to a pint,
sweeten with honey or loaf sugar, take a teaspoon full three times
a day. (UC)

[Aid for] Rattlesnake or Spider Bite

Take the yolk of an egg and stir in salt—as much as will make
it thick enough not to run off; spread a plaster and apply to the
wound. (UC)

Liniment

2 eggs well beaten, 1 pint of vinegar, 1/2 pint of turpentine. Put
in a bottle and mix well. Good for pains in body or limbs. (VC)

An Excellent Liniment

1 tablespoonfull of chloroform, one oz of sweet oil, as much of
gum camphor as the above will dissolve. (CC)

Remedy for Burns

The white of an egg, put on 7 or 8 times. Scraped Irish potato is also very good. (UC)

[Remedy for] Chapped Hands

A good remedy for chapped hands is to wash them in water slightly acidulated with vinegar or lemon juice, or wash them in milk. (VVC)

Cure for Earache

Put a little black pepper in some cotton and dip in sweet oil and insert into the ear. (UC)

Cure for Diptheria

1 teaspoonful of sulphur in some water used as a gargle. Also burn some in the house. (UC)

Rheumatism

1 drop caustic ammonia diluted in water taken internally will give almost instant relief. (UC)

Cure for Cancer

Melt as much lead as would make a bullet for a gun. While boiling it on the fire, stir in brimstone till it becomes finely powdered like flour, and the lead is all consumed. Now make the surface of the cancer sore (if there is not already a sore) by applying a fly plaster. Then put on so much of the powder that it can penetrate to the root of the cancer. Now cover with a linen cloth and keep dry. Repeat once or twice a day till the cancer is healed. This is communicated by Daniel Dillen Washington, Clinton, Ohio, July 1822. He further says by this remedy *I have healed many persons, never was unsuccessful, and I with confidence recommend it to my fellow citizens.* (UC)

Horse Founder [Cure]

Bleed copiously in the neck, bathe the legs well in warm water, dissolve a piece of alum (the size of an egg) in a pint of whiskey and a pint of water, and drench him with it; exercise him immediately after drenching. (CC)

Ed. note: This refers to when a horse was suffering from laminitis, inflammation of the hoof; it was also known as "founder."

3

TABLES

MANY SALEM KITCHENS featured a Dutch oven, which was a wall oven in which food was baked by utilizing its preheated brick walls. (The Salem Tavern kitchen rests on two levels—the level connected to the house is a raised platform with a brick floor; a staircase descends into the kitchen with its fireplace and cooking equipment.) Women cooked over an open fire; bread was baked in outside ovens.

Baking in a wood-fired oven required timing and experience. Comparing white-hot embers (about 550° to 600°F) to a "very low" oven is easy, but what about distinguishing the difference between "very hot" and "extremely hot"? Here's a conversion guide for temperatures along with other helpful weights, measures, and equivalents charts.

BAKE-OVEN TEMPERATURES
TO MODERN-DAY DEGREES

Very (s)low	250°–275°
Low	300°–325°
Moderate	350°–375°
Moderately hot	375°
Hot or quick	400°–425°
Very hot	450°–475°
Extremely hot	500°–525°

AVOIRDUPOIS WEIGHT

1 fluid drachm (dram) equals 1/8 fluid ounce or 3/4 teaspoon.
16 drachms equal 1 ounce.
16 ounces equal 1 pound.
25 pounds equal 1 quarter.
4 quarters equal 1 hundred.
20 hundred equal 1 ton.

WEIGHTS AND MEASURES

16 large tablespoonfuls make 1/2 pint or 1 cup.

8 large tablespoonfuls make 1 gill or 1/2 cup.

4 tablespoons (liquid) make 1 wineglass.

2 wineglasses make 1 gill.

1 round tablespoon butter makes 1 ounce.

4 teaspoonfuls of liquid make 1 tablespoonful.

4 teaspoonfuls of liquid make 1/2 gill or 1/4 a cup.

3 teaspoons (dry) make 1 tablespoon.

1 dessert spoon makes 2 teaspoons.

2 saltspoons make 1 coffee spoon.

2 coffee spoons make 1 teaspoon.

1 saltspoon makes 1/8 teaspoon.

1/2 a cup makes 1 gill.

2 gills make 1 cup (or 1/2 pint).

2 cups make 1 pint.

2 pints (4 cups) make 1 quart.

4 cups of flour make 1 quart.

4 cups of flour make 1 pound.

1/2 a cup of butter, solid, makes 1/4 pound, or 4 ounces.

2 cups of butter, solid, make 1 pound.

2 cups of granulated sugar make 1 pound.

2 1/2 cups of powdered sugar make 1 pound.

1 pint of milk or water makes 1 pound.

1 pint of chopped meat (solid) makes 1 pound.

10 eggs (without shells) make 1 pound.

8 eggs (with shells) make 1 pound.

2 tablespoonfuls of butter make 1 ounce.

4 tablespoonfuls of butter make 2 ounces or 1/4 a cup.

2 tablespoonfuls of granulated sugar make 1 ounce.

4 tablespoonfuls of flour make 1 ounce.

1 tablespoonful of liquid makes 1 ounce.

1 common-sized tumbler makes 1/2 gill or 4–6 fluid ounces.

60 drops make 1 teaspoon.

4 noggins make 1 pint.

1 cup butter (solid) makes 1/2 pound.

1 teacupful makes 4–6 fluid ounces.

1 coffee cup makes (roughly) 4/5 to 1 cup.

1 pottle makes 1/2 gallon.

1 hogshead of liquid makes one large cask (measuring from 63–140 gallons).

DRY MEASURE

2 pints equal 1 quart.
8 quarts equal 1 peck.
4 pecks equal 1 bushel.

LIQUID MEASURE

4 gills equal 1 pint.
2 pints equal 1 quart.
4 quarts equal 1 gallon.

USEFUL PROPORTIONS

1 measure of liquid to 1 measure of flour for pour batters.
1 measure of liquid to 2 measures of flour for drop batters.
1 measure of liquid to 3 measures of flour for dough.
1/2 to 2 or more cakes of compressed yeast softened in 1/2 cup
    of water to 1 pint of liquid.
1/2 cup of liquid yeast to 1 pint of liquid.
1 teaspoonful of soda and 3 1/2 teaspoonfuls of cream of tartar to
    one quart of flour.
1 teaspoonful of baking powder to 1 cup of flour.
1 teaspoonful of soda to 1 pint of thick sour milk.
1 teaspoonful of soda to 1 cup of molasses.
1/4 teaspoonful of salt to 1 quart of milk for custards.
1 teaspoonful of flavoring extract for a plain cake.
1 teaspoonful of flavoring extract to 1 quart of custard or cream.
1 tablespoonful of flavoring extract to 1 quart of mixture to be
    frozen.
2/3 cup or less of sugar to 1 quart of milk for custards.
1 cup of sugar to 1 quart of milk or cream for ice cream.
4 eggs to 1 quart of milk for plain custards.
6 to 8 eggs to 1 quart of milk for moulded custards.
1/4 package or half an ounce of gelatin to scant pint of liquid.
3 cups of water, more of milk or stock, to 1 cup of rice.
1 ounce (2 tablespoonfuls) of butter, 1/2 ounce (2 tablespoonfuls)
    of flour to 1 cup of liquid for soups.
1 ounce (2 tablespoonfuls) of butter, 1/2 ounce (2 tablespoonfuls)
    of flour to 1 cup of liquid for sauce.

4

BEVERAGES

As a rule, Salem inhabitants partook of four meals each day: breakfast, dinner, vesper, and supper. Vesper was their afternoon snack, usually served around three. Typical fare might include coffee and cake. If other Moravians were nearby, it might turn into a social gathering; this would usually become an opportunity to worship, as the participants would sing a hymn and offer thanks or petitions to God.

Strawberry Water Ice

One quart of strawberries, three fourths of a lb of sugar, juice of one lemon, one pint of hot water. Add the sugar and lemon to the berries; mash through a sieve, let stand one hour, add water, then freeze. (VC)

Soda Water

To 40 grams of carbonate of soda add 30 of taranic acid in small crystals. Fill a soda bottle with spring water, put in the mixture and cork it in [shantly?] with a well fitting cork. [It] ought to soak two or three hours before boiling. Roll lemons under your hand on a table to increase the quantity of juice. (VVC)

Vienna Coffee

Leach the coffee, allowing to each person a tablespoonful of ground coffee and 1 extra for the pot. Then to 1 quart of cream put into a [pot] and set in boiling water, allow the white of 1 egg and mix it well; remove the cream from the fire when hot and add the egg, stirring it briskly for a few seconds, then serve. (VVC)

Salem Board Minutes, Dec. 4, 1789

"Coffee shall be served at the Christmas lovefeast, instead of the tea hitherto used."[6]

Coffee holds a special place within Salem in the form of a huge coffee pot that has become a landmark in itself. Built in the 1850s as a means of attracting business, store owner Julius Mickey wanted to remind folks of his tin, roofing, and stove abilities. (If the pot were real, it has been said that it would hold just over 740 gallons of coffee.)

* * * * *

Ginger Pop

Mix 1 pound loaf sugar, 1 oz ground ginger, 1 oz cream tartar, and pour over them 1 gallon boiling water. Mix well, when nearly cold add one spoonful yeast, strain it, then bottle and tie down corks; it is ready for use six hours after making. (VC)

Receipt to Make Wild Grape Wine

3 lbs of sugar (brown) to 1 gallon of juice. Put in an open vessel, skim till quit [ ] working, say 8 or 10 days. Strain several times, then bottle it. (CC)

Blackberry Wine

To 1 gallon of blackberry juice add two gallons of water. To one gallon of this mixture add 3 pounds sugar, stir it well until all the sugar is melted, put it into a cask, not too full and lay the [bung?] loose on the hole; if it is put in bottles tie a muslin rag over it so that a little air can get in. In 4 weeks close it tight and about the latter part of October pour it off the yeast; it will now be fit for use. (UC)

Blackberry Cordial

2 quarts juice, 1 lb sugar, 1/2 oz nutmeg, 1/2 oz cinnamon, 1/2 oz cloves, 1/2 oz allspice, powdered. Boil 10 minutes and then add 1 pint brandy. French brandy is the best. Then boil a little and it is ready for use. (UC)

Extract from the Diary of Salem, 1835

"The national holiday was celebrated today with more than usual display but without noticeable disturbance. ...There was a celebration, in which there were cakes and drinks amid the sound of military music."[7]

To Make Raspberry Cordial

Take two quarts of raspberry juice, two pounds of good raisins, two pounds of loaf sugar, one pound of sugar, half an ounce of cinnamon, a few cloves, a little orange peel, and the juice of two large oranges; put all these ingredients in a gallon of brandy, stop it up in a stone jug; it will be fit for use in a week. (VVC)

Cherry Bounce

Take the juice of 1/2 bushel of cherries, and dissolve 24 lbs sugar above juice; put in a 40 gallon cask and fill up with whiskey. (CC)

To Make Syllabub

Take one pint of wine, sweeten it pretty sweet with loaf sugar, grate half a nutmeg in it, then milk the cow in the wine. (VVC)

Ginger Beer (William Grunert)

1 1/2 oz ginger bruised
1 oz cream tartar
1 lb loaf sugar
1 sliced lemon

Put in a pan and pour six qu[arts] of boiling water upon them; when nearly cold put in a little yeast and stir for a minute. Let stand till next day. Then strain and bottle. Should be kept in a cool place with corks well tied down. Fit for use in 3 days. (CC)

Good Beer (E.W. Lineback)

To 1 gallon water take 1 pint molasses—is best to boil it. If boiled, let it cool off. Then add rivals not quite a tablespoon full dissolved. Let stand 10 or 12 hours, then bottle in warm weather. Fit for use in 12 hours. Add 1 tablespoonful ginger. (CC)

5

VEGETABLES, FRUITS & SIDE DISHES

T HE TYPICAL SALEM Moravian home included a bounteous vegetable garden that was planted behind the house (larger farms existed on the outer fringes of the village; many families also had more extensive plots there where they could grow field crops).

Many things both wild and cultivated grew in Salem, providing a varied diet for its citizens. Early on, they found that many things were growing well: "mulberries (black), persimmon tree (persummens), plums, wild cherries (black and small, but edible), elderberries (good to eat raw), grape-vines are the most plentiful (blue, red, white {rare}, Fox Grapes {Bottom wine is made}, Upland Grapes {"the best" various wines and vinegar made from it}), brambleberries (Brumbeeren), raspberries (Himbeeren), hazel nuts, hops, bug root (bear blackberries), sumach (a rich, red, shrublike plant with broad leaves the Indians smoke like tobacco)... The wood is a good, black dye. Ink can also be made from it."

They categorized the following list of fruit trees: "apple (many), pear (few), peaches (many), apricots (few), sweet cherries (few), sour cherries (few), white grapes, gooseberries, garden currants, clove gilliflower, roses, privet."

Cultivated plants and grains were also in abundance: "anise, beans of all kinds, red cabbage, coriander, cucumber, dill, peas, flax, barley, garden rhubarb, yellow turnips, oats, hops, hoarhound, cabbage, all kinds, mint, garlic, head lettuce, caraway, rye, cress, pumpkins, Irish potatoes, valerian, leek, lavender, marjoram, poppy, milk thistle, watermelons, mush melons, Neyer Corn (grows like Indian corn, but the grain is more like rice and bitter. It's planted for use in making brooms), parsnips, sweet potatoes, rosemary, radishes, turnips, rice, sage, Spanish cress, chives, spinach, store peas, asparagus, sunflower, white grapes, tobacco, wheat, corn, hyssop, sugar peas, onions...and several mushroom (edible)..."[8]

In the early days of Salem, tomatoes weren't grown because they were thought to be poisonous; nevertheless, in years to come tomatoes were introduced into various dishes. (Tomatoes reportedly became popular in America in the early 1800s.) Conversely, not a single recipe includes mushrooms—there was no reliable guide in the eighteenth or nineteenth century that distinguished edible varieties from the poisonous ones.

Tip for Good Vegetables

* Should be as fresh as it is practical, and get them well cooked.

* Potatoes should not stop boiling for an instant; when done turn off the water and throw in a little salt to absorb the remaining moisture.

* Cabbage takes at least an hour.

* Cauliflower: Separate the green part and cut the flower close at the bottom of the stalk. Let it soak an hour in boiling milk and water or water, skimming well. When it feels tender, it should be instantly taken up. Drain and serve with melted butter. (VVC)

To Plant Asparagus

Sow early in spring, thinly, in shallow drills about one foot apart. Before sowing, the seed should be soaked 24 hours in tepid water. When one or two years old, dig beds two feet deep, mixing in plenty of manure in which transplant the roots in drills fifteen inches apart and one foot apart in drill. (CC)

Hulled Corn is Prepared as Follows

Put the corn (shelled of course) into an iron kettle, with a bag of ashes sufficient to make a pretty strong lye, add water, and boil until the hulls or skins of the corn separate and rise to the top, whence they are to be skimmed; then take out the corn, and boil slowly in fair water, with a little salt, till tender. It is eaten with sugar. (VVC)

To Can Corn

Select ears right for table use, husk, put in boiling water and boil 10 minutes. Take out, cut from cob, lay on cloths. Spread on a tin roof to dry, stirring frequently. When quite dry in two days, put in a bag and hang in sun or wind a day or two, then hang up away till wanted. When needed, wash the quantity required. Soak overnight in sufficient water to cook. Pour the water the next day into a stew pan and when scalding hot put in the corn. Stew it gently 20 minutes. Put in seasoning and a little cream. (VVC)

What Makes a Bushel

Wheat, sixty pounds
Corn, shelled, fifty-six pounds
Corn, on the cob, seventy pounds
Rye, fifty pounds
Oats, thirty-six
Barley, forty-six
Buckwheat, fifty-two
Irish potatoes, sixty
Sweet potatoes, fifty
Onions, fifty-seven

Beans, sixty
Bran, twenty
Cloverseed, sixty
Timothy seed, forty-five
Flax, forty-five
Hemp seed, forty-five
Blue grass seed, fourteen
Dried peaches, thirty-three
(VVC)

Potato Dish

Boil potatoes and let them cook, then cut them in rather thick slices. Put a lump of butter in a stew pan and add a little flour, about a teaspoonful for a middle-sized dish. When the flour has boiled a little, while in the water add by degrees a cupful of broth or water; when this has boiled up, put in the potatoes with parsley, pepper, and salt. Let potatoes stew a few minutes; take them from the fire and when quit off the boil, add the yolk of 1 egg beat up with lemon juice of a tablespoonful of cold water—as soon as the sauce is set, bring to table. (VVC)

Irish Potato Dumpling to Put with Sour Kraut

Mash your potatoes very fine, then stir in flour, two eggs, salt, and water. Make a tolerable soft dough, then dip out with a spoon into boiling salt water and let them boil until done. (UC)

Southern Mode of Boiling Rice

Pick and rinse it well in cold water, drain off the water, then put it in a pot of boiling water with a little salt. 1 pint of water to a teacup of rice, as it absorbs the water very much while boiling. Boil 17 minutes then turn the water off very close, set the pot over a few coals and let it steam 15 minutes with the lid of the pot off. The beauty of the rice boiled in this way is that each kernel stands out by itself, while it is quite tender. (VVC)

Apple Snow

Bake six large apples; when cold scrape the pulp and put in a bowl with one teacup of sugar and the white of one egg; beat to a snow. (VC)

Reserved Apples

Select large fair tart apples, pare them thin and if you prefer them whole, core them or cut them in halves. Take out the core. Allow 3/4 lb sugar to 1 lb apples. Boil until the fruit is clear and tender. Remove each piece when done. They will require equal weight of sugar if intended to keep long, still less may be used if to be eaten immediately. A few slices of lemon or sticks of candy boiled in the syrup improves the flavor. (UC)

To Cook Prunes

So take prunes, soak them in warm water until they soften a bit. Take the stones out and instead put in shelled sweet almonds. Make a batter, as for pancakes, but instead of the milk, take beer and stir the batter with that. Put the prunes in, turn to coat, and cook in melted butter. (Note: If you're doing this with apples, use the dough suitable for apple pie). (WC)

Testing Eggs

There is no difficulty whatever in testing eggs. Take them into a room moderately dark and hold them between the eye and a candle or lamp. If the egg is good, that is if the albumen is still unaffected, the light will shine through with a reddish glow, while if the egg is affected it will be opaque or dark. A very few trials will show anyone the ease and simplicity of this method. (VVC)

THE EASTER SUNRISE SERVICE

MORAVIANS BEGAN what has become a Christian-wide tradition of holding an Easter sunrise service. Even above the festive celebration of Christmas, Moravians esteem Easter as the pivotal and essential reality of the Christian faith. The first sunrise service was impromptu, but was proclaimed so uplifting that it developed into an annual ritual for the entire congregation. Salem's first Easter sunrise service was held in 1773. Virtually the same Easter Litany used then is still used today.

As with other Moravian rituals, music was integral throughout the service. Band members would rise early, walking through the streets as they played hymns to awaken citizens before sunrise. In later years, band members were treated to a breakfast of ham and eggs and coffee in return for their service.

Omelet

6 eggs, beaten separately, 1/2 teacup of cracker crumbs, 4 1/2 cups of sweet milk all mixed together, and fried in a little hot butter. It cannot be turned to brown on top in the oven. (VC)

Egg Dumplings

1 pt of milk, 2 eggs, 1 teaspoon salt, flour enough to make a batter as thick as for pound cake; have a clean sauce pan of boiling water, let the water boil fast, drop in the batter by tablespoons. 4 to 5 minutes will boil them. Put a bit of butter and pepper over and serve with boiled or cold meat or for a dessert sauce. (VVC)

6

DRESSINGS, GRAVIES, SAUCES & CREAMS

[Cookery Etiquette]

Never pour melted butter over anything but send to table in a sauce tureen or boat. (VVC)

Drawn or Melted Butter

Rub in two teaspoonfuls of flour into a quarter of a pound of butter. Add five teaspoonfuls of cold water. Set it into boiling water and let it melt, and heat until it begins to simmer, and it is done. Never simmer it on coals, as it fries the oil and spoils it. Be careful not to have the flour in lumps... (VVC)

Drawn Butter

Mix two tablespoonfuls of butter and a tablespoonful of flour to a smooth paste in a bowl, set in boiling water, thin with a teacupful of boiling water, stir until thick, add a pinch of salt. Take from the fire and serve. (VVC)

Lemon Butter

To 1 lemon, 1 cup sugar, 2 eggs, a lump of butter, grate the rinds, take the juice, boil all a few minutes. (UC)

[Van Vleck] Lemon Butter

One and a half cups of granulated sugar, the juice of two lemons and the grated rind of one, three eggs, the whites and yolks beaten separately, butter the size of a walnut. Boil the lemons, sugar, yolks, and butter together over a slow fire, stirring constantly. Beat the whites until very stiff and stir in when cool. This may be used for sandwiches or put on the table in a small glass dish. (VVC)

Delicious Lemon Sauce

Beat 2 tablespoons butter, 1 cup sugar, 1 teaspoonful flour. Add 1/2 a cup boiling water. Cook till clear. Flavor to taste with the juice and part of the grated rind. (VVC)

Lemon Sauce

This recipe is written across a 1906 Owens Drug Company form letter. The drugstore was at the corner of Main Street and Third Street at the front of Zinzendorf Hotel.

Boil 2 tablespoons butter
1 cup white sugar
1 teaspoon flour cornstarch
1/2 cup boiling water
Cook till clear. Flavor juice and rind of lemon (grated). (VVC)

Standing Sauce for the Kitchen

1 quart Claret or white wine—put in a glazed pan the juice of 2 lemons, pepper, ginger, mace, cloves, lemon peel, and put them in a bag and put this in the wine. Stop it close and set in hot water for 1 hour. Keep in a warm place. A spoonful is good in any sauce. (VVC)

A Good [Soft] Sauce

Cream together 1 cup of pulverized sugar and 1 half cup of fresh butter. Add a well beaten egg and juice and grated peel of lemon. Have ready a double saucepan for some boiling water which has been previously thickened with a scant teaspoonful of corn starch. When thoroughly boiling add to this your other ingredients and stir slowly till the sauce is very hot. Add a little grated nutmeg and it is done. (VVC)

Wine Sauce

Have ready some rich thick melted or drawn butter and the moment you take it from the fire stir in powdered sugar and nutmeg. Serve it up with plum pudding or any sort of boiled pudding that is made of butter. Add wine. A teacup sugar, the same butter, teaspoonful flour. When a smooth paste, gradually [add] into it 1 pint boiling water, stir for 10 minutes over the fire; add wine or lemon or vinegar before it leaves the fire. (VVC)

Mint Sauce

Young and green mint, the leaves chopped fine and mixed with cold vinegar, and a teaspoonful of sugar. Enough vinegar to moisten but not to make liquid. Serve with roast lamb. (VVC)

Parsley Sauce

Wash a bunch of parsley in cold water—then boil 6–7 minutes in salt water. Drain and chop fine. Have ready some melted butter and stir in the parsley 2 small tablespoonfulls to 1/2 pint butter. To boiled fowls, pork, fish, and other boiled fresh fish. Apple, peach, and cranberry to serve with a roasted fowl and meats. Cranberry may be moulded in pretty forms and brought to table in glass plates. (VVC)

Bread Sauce

Put grated bread into a sauce pan and pour over them some of the liquor in which poultry or fresh meat has been boiled (in water and butter). Add some plums or dried currants, having simmered till the bread is soft and the currants plump. Add butter or cream. (VVC)

Egg Sauce

Boil 4 eggs for an hour. Dip them into cold water to prevent their turning blue. Peel off the shell. Chop the yolks of all, the whites of 2, and stir into melted butter. Serve with boiled poultry or fish. (VVC)

Celery Sauce

A large bunch cut in pieces and boilt gently in a small quantity of beaten till quite tender. Season it. Take a tolerable large lump of butter, roll it in flour and stir into the sauce. Boil again and it is ready for table. It may also be made of cream instead of water, 1/2 pint to a walnut size of butter—nutmeg and mace. Eat with boilt poultry. (VVC)

Brown Onion Sauce

Slice the onions, cover with butter, and set them over a slow fire. Add salt, cayenne, brown gravy thickened with a lump of butter rolled in flour that has first been browned by holding it on a hot pan. For roasted poultry, game, or meat. (VVC)

Chile Sauce

4 dozen large ripe tomatoes, peeled, 4 onions, chopped fine, 5 green peppers, 4 tablespoons of salt (even), 4 tablespoons of sugar (heaped), 3 teacups of good strong vinegar. Boil down half. (VC)

Gravies and Sauces...

To brown butter: Put 2 ounces butter into a frying pan over a small fire; when melted, dust in a little flour and keep stirring it till thick and brown. (VVC)

A Salad Dressing

To a cup of vinegar put a teaspoonful of oil, with the same of [ ] mustard, and a saltspoon of salt, rub the yolk of a hardboiled egg smooth and add it to the dressing; beat them well together, then pour it over the celery or other salad. (VVC)

Receipt for Making Citron Melon

Cut and pare your rind: to 2 lb. of rind take 1 oz of alum, and boil them together twenty minutes; let them remain in the alum water 6 hours; then make a strong Ginger Tea, and boil the rind in it 20 minutes, then let it lay in your Ginger Tea for 8 hours. Prepare your syrup by taking 2 lbs. of double refined sugar to 1 lb. of rind. Add ginger and Essence of Lemon to suit your taste. (VVC)

To Make Raspberry Cream

Take a quart of sweet rich cream, let it just boil, take it up, stir it until it is almost cold, put into it some raspberry juice to your taste, stir all one way for a quarter of an hour, sweeten to your taste and serve it up. (VVC)

Cold Sweet Sauce

Stir together as for a pound cake equal quantities of fresh butter and sugar. When quite light and creamy add cinnamon or nutmeg and a few drops of essence of lemon. Eat to puddings, dumplings and fritters, pancakes. (VVC)

The Best Kind of Catsup

is made from <u>tomatoes</u>. They should be squeezed up in the hand, salt put to them and set by for 24 hours. After being baked [and run] through a sieve, cloves, allspice, pepper, mace, garlic, and whole mustard seed should be added. It should be boiled down one third and bottled after it is cool. The garlic should be taken out before it is bottled. (VVC)

Tomato Catsup

1 gallon ripe tomatoes, 1 tablespoon salt, four of ground pepper, 3 mustard, 1 teaspoon allspice, 1 of cloves, 1 of cinnamon, 6 little red peppers, simmer the whole slowly with a pint of vinegar for 3 or 4 hours. Strain through a sieve, cork tight. (VC)

Cucumber Catchup

Take 3 doz full grown cucumbers and 8 onions. Peal the onions and cucumbers and chop them as fine as possible. Sprinkle on 3/4 of a pint salt, put the whole in a sieve and let it drain well. Then take a teacup of mustard seed, 1/2 teacup of ground black pepper, and mix well with the cucumbers and onions then put in bottles or jars and fill up with strong vinegar and close up well. In 3 days it is fit for use. (UC)

7

BREADS

YEAST AND BREAD

From a newspaper clipping dated 1886.

This is the poetry of bread, said my cousin to me,
May I ask your good cook how to make it? said she.
If you choose, I replied, but you had better ask me.
Of course my cook made it, that's certainly true,
But I taught her to do it—and I can teach you.
If with the yeast you would like to begin,
Sew a handful of hops a small bag within;
Boil it in two quarts of water ten minutes or less,
Till the strength is extracted—you can tell by a guess.
Then like a poor thing that has had its best day,
You may squeeze out the hop-bag and throw it away.
Put six nice peeled potatoes in that boiling hot water
And keep it boiling—not faster than it "oughter"—
Till the potatoes are soft, then take from the fire;
Add a tablespoonful of salt, and one of sugar you'll desire.
Mash the potatoes all fine with a masher or spatter,
Put in handfuls of flour till it makes a thick batter.
Then let it cool slowly till lukewarm, at least,
Now add half a cake of dissolved compressed yeast.
In a few hours this mixture will be all in a bubble.
It is excellent yeast without very much trouble.
Then by adding corn-meal till a stiff dough it makes,
You can roll it out nicely and cut it in cakes.
When carefully drying turn every cake over,
Till each and every side is as dry as the other.
In the making of bread I've respect for the eater,
And will not risk the bread for the sake of a metre.
Good bread is a necessity, as every one knows,
So I will give all directions in the plainest of prose... (VVC)

To Make Yeast

To two middling sized boiled potatoes, add a [pint] <u>boiling</u> water and two tablespoonfulls of brown sugar. One pint of hot water should be applied to every 1/2 pint of the compound. Hot water is better in warm weather. This yeast being made without flour will keep longer and is said to be much better than any previously in use. (VVC)

Yeast

Peal 1 large potato, boil till soft, rub it through a sieve, add an equal quantity of flour, make it sufficiently liquid with hop tea and when a little warmer than new milk, add a gill of yeast— stir it well and keep it close.

Another way:
I double a handful of hops, boil them in 2 gallons water to one, then take 1/2 tb rye flour, 1/4 tb sugar, 4 eggs mixed in a thin batter with water; pour this in the hop water while boiling on the fire. Let it give one boil up, take it off, and when cold, put it in a jug for use. (VVC)

Liquid Yeast

1/2 gallon of boiling water
1/2 pint hot tea
1/2 cup sugar
1/2 cup salt
5 large potatoes boiled and mashed through the colunder. Good 1/2 pint of yeast. (VC)

Biscuit

3 pints flour, 1 pint milk, 1 small cup of shortening, if you take lard it must be less than butter, 3 teaspoons of cream of tartar, 1 1/2 of soda. Mix the cream of tartar with the flour first, then rub the lard in the flour until the whole is thoroughly mixed. Melt the soda in the milk, sour milk is best, then add the milk and work it very well, [roll] out and bake quick. (UC)

Souffle Biscuit

Rub 4 ounces butter, 1 [pint] flour, make it in to paste with milk, knead it well, roll it as thin as paper, and bake it to look white. (VVC)

UNLIKE TYPICAL SETTLEMENTS, Salem's economic development was completely tied to the church. Moravian elders were involved in all aspects of the town and acted as its governing body under God. The communal system, which encouraged each person to contribute according to talent and ability, discouraged business competition; elders were careful to place the best person with each livelihood. An experienced baker, Christian Winkler bought the bakery in Salem in 1808, and he and family members operated it for more than a century.

The Winkler Bakery is still in use today as part of Old Salem, and visitors can tour the building as well as buy baked goods. Its oven continues to be heated with wood, as it was when Christian Winkler wrote the following:

"THE CONFECTIONER'S SHOP"
{BY CHRISTIAN WINKLER}

"ORDERLINESS AND HOSPITALITY must prevail in any business. With the confectioner as well, these virtues must not be missing. There are in his shop, in his trade, all sorts of waste, of sugar, sugar dust, and crumbs, which after the finished product remain behind on the table, in pans, and in mortars. In the preparation of macaroons, biscuits, and other sorts of baked goods which are baked on paper, there usually remains at the end something stuck [to the vessels or implements], many pieces of ware are broken in pieces, much is spoiled or becomes too old. What a shame for the confectioner if he does not know the means to take advantage of these by-products. One has a special box, not only in the laboratory but also in the shop, to save these waste pieces. ...One stores macaroons, confections, etc., as we once for all recall, most practically in dry places in glass containers." (WC)

Sweet Biscuits

Rub 4 ounces butter well into 8 ounces flour, add 6 ounces of loaf sugar, the yolks of 2 eggs and the white of 1, and a tablespoon of brandy. Roll the paste thin and cut it with a wine glass or cutter, egg over the tops with the remaining white and sift on white sugar. Bake it in a warm oven. (VVC)

Butter Biscuits

2 pounds flour, 3/4 pound butter, 1/2 pint milk or cold water, and salt. (VVC)

Risen Biscuits

1 quart of milk, 3/4 cup butter and lard (half and half), 3/4 cup of yeast, 2 tablespoons white sugar, 1 of salt, flour enough to make a soft dough. Mix overnight warming the milk and melting the lard and butter. In the morning roll out into a sheet, cut in round cakes, let them rise for 20 minutes and bake 20 minutes. (VC)

Butter Crackers

Mm. Dixon

To 1 pint sour milk take 3/4 pound butter, 1 teaspoon full soda; work it and pound with an ax. (VVC)

Butter Roll

So take 1/2 cup fresh butter. Let it melt and stir it with 6 eggs into a froth. Then stir white flour into it until it is a stiff dough. Set fresh milk on the fire, and when it is boiling put the dough in it in pieces the size of a walnut, and let it cook a little. Then take them out of the milk and put onto a platter and bake in the oven or cake pan. (WC)

The Best of Rolls

2 quarts of flour, 2 tablespoonfuls of butter rubbed into the flour. Make a hole in the flour and pour in 1 pint of cold boiled milk, half a teacup yeast. Let it stand just so till morning, then knead 15 minutes. Let it rise till noon, then make into rolls and let them rise till tea time. Bake 20 minutes in a hot oven. (UC)

Salem Diary
July 1, 1789

"We think with praise and thanksgiving of the goodness of God who has blessed our fields and meadows with a bountiful harvest, and fine weather for the harvest."[9]

Potatoe Bread

1 quart of flour, 1 cup of finely mashed sweet potatoes, a piece of butter the size of an egg, a small portion of yeast, make up and set to rise an hour or so before baking. Roll it into cakes a little larger than a biscuit, and let it rise again then bake quick. (UC)

Bread Dumplings

So take a large roll. Grate it with a grate, or soak it in fresh water and then squeeze the water out again. [Take] a 1/4 cup fresh butter. Let it melt and stir it with 5 eggs to a froth. Put in a little salt and mace with the roll, and make a stiff dough of it. Set water on the fire, and when it is boiling, then with a spoon make pieces about the size of a walnut until the dough is all [ ] and drop them in one after the other. Let them cook until done. Then put brown butter over them. (WC)

Spanish Buns

1 cup butter, 1 cup sweet milk, 3 cups sugar, 4 eggs, 1 teaspoon soda, 2 cream tartar, 1 tablespoon sweet wine, 1 tablespoon brandy, 1/2 lb raisins, 1/4 lb citron, 1/4 lb currents, 4 cups flour.

Ed. note: It originally had "4 or 5 cups flour," but later she crossed through "or 5." (UC)

[Vogler] Spanish Buns

One cup butter (heaped), 1 of sweet milk, 3 of sugar, 1 teaspoon soda, 2 tablespoons brandy, 4 eggs, 1/2 nutmeg, 1/2 raisins, 1/4 pound currants, citron, 4 or 5 cups flour to be added last. Bake like sugar cake. (VC)

[Van Vleck] Spanish Buns

1 cup butter, 1 cup sweet milk, 1 teaspoon soda dissolved in the milk, 3 cups sugar, 4 eggs, 2 tablespoons brandy, 1/2 pound raisins, 1/4 pound currants, some citron, 1/2 nutmeg, 4 or 5 cups flour which must go in last. (VVC)

Indian Corn and Wheat Flour Bread

Take 1 quart of cornmeal to a little salt and 1 quart of boiling water. Wet the meal, let it stand until it be bloodwarm, then add 2 quarts of wheat flour and 1/2 pint yeast and let it rise. This quantity will make two loaves. Bake it 1 1/2 hours. (VVC)

Egg Corn Bread

3 eggs, 3 pints buttermilk, 1 teaspoon soda, butter or lard the size of an egg, melted, meal to make a thin batter, bake in a tin well greased and hot. (UC)

Corn Batter Cakes

2 eggs, 1 quart buttermilk, 1 teaspoon soda, butter if you like, salt to taste, meal to make a tolerable thin batter, put in the soda last. (UC)

Waffles

1 quart flour, 2 eggs, 1 teaspoon soda, put enough buttermilk to make a thin batter, a little salt. (UC)

Mrs. Jones Receipt for Waffles

This wonderful handwritten receipt is dated 1877.

1 cup milk
3 well beaten eggs
1 tablespoonful melted butter
1 teaspoonful cream tartar
1/2 teaspoonful soda
1/2 teaspoonful salt
a heaping pint of flour
If you have buttermilk use the same quantity of that instead of sweet milk and no cream tartar. (VVC)

Griddle Cakes

Use milk altogether and no water. Two eggs, yellow and white, to be allowed for 1 pint of cornmeal, the milk to be a little warmed and the whole to be well beaten with a spoon. There must be milk enough to make it liquid enough to be poured out. 1 spoonful of wheat flour and butter the size of a walnut. (VVC)

Delicious Johnnycakes

This recipe was written on the back of a quarterly statement dated April 1, 1881.

1 egg
2 spoonfuls sugar
a piece butter (size of a walnut)
2 cups sour milk
1 teaspoonful soda
Beat well and add Indian meal enough to make a thin batter. Bake in [ ] pan in a hot oven. (VVC)

Gardens within Salem were known throughout the region for their stellar crops. Perhaps John Christian Blum had a hand in this; in 1828, he began publishing the famous Blum's Almanac, *which continues even now as the guide by which to plant. The almanac, geared toward "the signs" of the sun, moon, and stars, provides vital information of what times of year to plant (and avoid planting) seeds.*

* * * * *

Indian Muffins

Pour boiling water into 1 quart of cornmeal, stir it well to a thick batter; when cooled a little, add a tablespoonful of yeast, 2 eggs well beaten, and 1 teaspoonful salt. Set it in a warm place to rise for 2 hours—then butter square tin pans, fill them 2/3rds full, and bake in a quick oven. (VVC)

Ginger Bread

1 cup of molasses, 1 cup of sugar, 3 cups of flour, 3 eggs, 1 teaspoon of soda, 1 cup of sour milk, 1 teaspoon ginger, 1 of cinnamon, 1/2 cup lard. (VC)

Ginger-bread

Mrs. Hay

2 cups Molasses, 1 cup sugar, 1 cup buttermilk, 1 tablespoonful of soda, 1 of beat ginger, 6 eggs, 5 light cups flour, 2 cups butter <u>or</u> 1 1/2 of lard. (UC)

Loaf Ginger Bread

3 eggs, 1 teacup of molasses, 1 and 1 1/2 teacups of sugar, 1 teacup of lard, 1 teacup of sour milk, 5 teacups of flour, 2 tablespoons of ginger, 1 tablespoon of soda dissolved in boiling water. (VC)

Soft Ginger Bread

Half cup of sugar, one cup of molasses, half cup of butter, one teaspoon each of ginger, cinnamon, and cloves, two teaspoons soda dissolved in one cup of boiling water, two and one-half cups of flour; add two well-beaten eggs the last thing before baking. This is excellent. (VVC)

Baben

2 pounds bread dough, 1/2 lb of butter, 1/2 lb sugar, 3 eggs, cinnamon to your taste. (UC)

Luncheon Cake

Make a sponge of a pint of lukewarm water into which stir as much flour as will make a thick batter. Add a little salt and a cupful of homemade yeast. Have a pound of dried currants nicely washed and a 1/4 of a pound of raisins stoned. Flour the fruit and add to the sponge when light. Stir together 1/2 pound of sugar with 3 ounces of butter. Add this with 1 pound of flour to the other ingredients and as much milk as will make a soft dough; knead it well and put in a pan. Let it rise again and bake it in a moderate oven. (VVC)

Pint Cake

1 pint dough, 1 teaspoon sugar, 1 cup butter, 3 eggs, 1 teaspoon soda. (VC)

Ed. note: Later within the original receipt book, this recipe is repeated except *it reads to use "1 teacup of sugar, 1 teacup butter, 3 eggs beaten separately"; the dough and the soda remain the same.*

LOVEFEAST

ONE OF MORAVIANS' most revered and distinctive rituals is the service that is dedicated to the greatest of Christian virtues: love. Dating back to Germany and held throughout the church year in connection with holidays and days of church significance, lovefeast is a common meal partaken in love and fellowship; the basis for this practice is described within Chapter 2 of Acts. As with most Moravian customs, the service emphasizes music and hymns. Lovefeast consists of a plain sweet bun and, currently, coffee (which replaced tea in 1789), and every person present is served. This was another way in which the Salem congregation conducted itself as a collective family, breaking bread together. It is one of the church's significant and enduring ways of materially sharing the bounty and love of God with others. The Moravian blessing is prayed in unison:

Come, Lord Jesus,
Our Guest to be,
And bless these gifts,
Bestowed by Thee.
Amen.

In recent years, the following lines have been added to the original table grace:

Bless Thy dear ones everywhere,
And keep them in Thy loving care.

Moravian Love Feast Buns

For one-half gallon of sponge, two cakes yeast, one-half gallon sweet milk, one-half gallon warm water, 2 lbs sugar, 3 oz salt, a little mace and cinnamon. Mix at night to be used next day. This will make 180 2-oz cakes. (UC)

The Diary of the Congregation in Salem, May 14, 1781

"There is only enough sugar left for one lovefeast, and if no more comes in this will be saved for the lovefeast of the little boys."[10]

*   *   *   *   *

"Salem clings to its toue of the seventeenth century....Here are seen some peculiar customs that the Moravians perpetuate. One of these is the practice of holding 'love-feasts.' In these a service of song is held, during which a bun and a mug of coffee are served to each worshiper, to be eaten and drunk while the choir sings an anthem. On Christmas eve two lovefeasts are held—one for the adults in the evening, and in the afternoon one for the children. At the children's feast, after the mugs are carried away, the lights are lowered and lighted wax tapers are distributed among the little folks. The minister, holding his own taper, tells of the Saviour who heralded the coming of light to all the world, and then, through the dusk, the tiny beads of flame flit across the old square as each child endeavors to carry his taper home still lighted. There are other festivals and anniversary occasions that are peculiar to these people, who have managed to perpetuate the zeal of the earliest settlers amid the confusing discord of the active affairs of this era...."

Excerpted from a circa 1896 *Harpers Weekly* article by Julian Ralph, "The Very Old and Very New at Winston [and] Salem."

Formula for Love Feast Buns

1 gal base—water

2 lb butter
1 lb shortening
3 lbs 8 oz sugar
1/2 oz nutmeg
1/2 oz mace
juice and gratings 1 orange, 1 lemon
6 oz malt
5 oz salt

Cream the above lightly.

1 lb 8 ozs whole eggs add while creaming
1 lb yeast dissolve in part of the 1 gallon water
5 lbs pastry flour
11 lbs 8 oz bread flour

Temperature 80, rest 1 hour.

Punch and let rest just long enough to round up good. 15 to pan like sandwich rolls. Let prove enough to recede nicely when pressed out with board. Do not knock down at this stage too sudden after they are down you can pat them to desired diameter without damage at this stage; dip letter M in melted butter and stamp bun in top M or cut with razor blade /-/-/-/. Let rise again and bake at about 400 degrees or to nice reddish brown. [Scaling weight to piece four and one half or 2 oz to each bun.] (UC)

Sugar Cake

1 quart of yeast, 1 quart milk, 2 cups of butter, 2 cups sugar, 4 eggs, 1 teaspoon soda, [flour?]. (VC)

Moravian Sugar Cake

2 cups of bread rising, 1 pint of milk, salt to taste, 1 cup of butter or butter and fresh lard, 1 cup sugar, thoroughly worked as stiff as bread dough and until it will not adhere to the fingers. Let it [rise] in a warm place and when light, spread it about an inch thick on tins and let it rise again. When very light, punch holes at equal distances, cover with moist brown sugar, and lay small pieces of butter on so that it will melt with the sugar into the holes. Sprinkle with cinnamon and bake in a rather quick oven for 15 or 20 minutes. (UC)

While Salem depended on its surroundings for some raw materials and food, organized trips to other towns were still regular occurrences to bring in foodstuffs not available locally. Charleston and Philadelphia were some of the favored trade centers to buy such supplies as tea, coffee, sugar, and other nonedible goods that were then resold to individuals.

* * * * *

[Vogler] Sugar Cake

1 cup mashed potatoes, 1 cup brown sugar, when cool enough stir in 1 cup of rivels. Let stand until morning and add 1 cup warm sweet milk, 1 cup melted lard, 1 egg. Makes a large cake. (VC)

Mrs. Dettman's Sugar Cake

"Receipt with liquid yeast."

Filling for cake: 2 1/2 cups of brown sugar, 3/4 cup of cream, 1 tablespoon of butter. Boil until thick. Let it cool a little, flavor with vanilla and spread between and over the cake.

---

1 cup of sweet milk, 1 large pint of yeast, 5 ounces sugar, 5 ounces butter or lard, 2 eggs. Make a good dough but not as stiff as bread dough, about 2 quarts of flour. 1/2 of the receipt is enough for a small family. (VC)

Moravian Cake

1 teacup of yeast, 1 of sugar, 1 of mashed Irish potatoes, 1 teacup milk, 1 of lard, 1 egg. In the evening put the yeast, sugar, and potatoes together. In the morning add the milk, lard, and egg, and make up your dough. (UC)

8

MEATS

General Remarks on Meat

* It should be carefully washed and dried with a clean towel before it is cooked.

* Frozen meat should not be cooked the same day but soaked in cold water first. When meat is to be kept any time it should be carefully wiped every day.

* Mutton and venison are best after keeping several days.

* Pork should be thoroughly cooked. But is thought best when not quite done. (VVC)

Economy in Meat

Take cold meat of any kind—pieces left from the table; cut in pieces a quarter of an inch square; put in a frying pan; cover the meat with water; put in a small piece of butter, pepper, and salt; when this comes to a boil, stir in a little flour and water, previously mixed. Have two or three slices of bread toasted; place them on a platter. Pour over them the meat and gravy while hot. This will be found an excellent dish prepared from meat usually thrown away. (VVC)

To Dry Beef

For 100 pounds of beef, make a brine of nine pounds of salt, two pounds of brown sugar, one quart of molasses, two ounces of saltpetre, two ounces of saleratus. Mix them well together in water then boil and skim; when this is cool pour it over the meat, being careful to have every particle well covered. Let the beef remain in the brine until the seasoning has [soaked?] thro' it then take it out, wipe dry, and hang it up; when sufficient dry it may be enclosed in bags, tight that no insect can enter; keep in a cool dry place; it may be smoked for a day or two or longer if desired, as hams are smoked. (CC)

To Cure Beef

Take 4 gallons water, add one pound of brown sugar, one pint molasses, 2 oz nitre, and salt enough to float an egg; this is enough for one common quarter of beef. (CC)

Oats with Sourleaf to Cook [with Broth]

One checks over the oats, then wash them well and soak them in hot water. Take beef broth and put it in a soup pot with onion, whole nutmeg, and let this cook a little. Your oats should be added to the broth. Don't add much of it, then add the sourleaf to the broth, which has been well washed, then added to the oats and a little bit of fresh butter, salt it a little and stir in a beaten egg yolk and a little sweet cream and pour it over bread slices. (UC)

[Untitled]

1 lb and 1/2 of ground beef
1 cup of crackers ground
1 cup of sweet milk
1 egg, salt, and pepper
Bake 3/4 of an hour. (VC)

Beef Steaks

Have the gridiron perfectly clean and heat over a clean [ ] fire; lay on the meat and turn constantly; throw a little salt over. Serve as hot as possible without gravy or with a dab of butter on them.

Another way:
A tender piece an inch thick put on hot coals 15 minutes, turning frequently without sticking in them with the fork—when almost done take butter, pepper, salt; lay it on the gridiron for about 2 minutes, turning once. Take off and add butter. The best are cut from the ribs. Improved by beating. (VVC)

Steaks

Sprinkle salt on the coals. When the gridiron is quite hot, rub it with fat, sprinkle a little salt over the coals, 1/2 hour is generally enough. When one side is done cover with the inverted side of a plate. When dry sprinkle salt and pepper, lay on a hot dish and put on a lump of butter when almost done or take butter, pepper, salt, lay it on the grid iron for about 2 minutes, turning once. Take off and add butter. (VVC)

Roast Beef

When the meat is first put on, a little salt should be sprinkled on it and the bony side turned toward the greatest heat. When the bones get well heated through, turn the meat and keep a brisk fire—baste it frequently while roasting a little water when you put the meat in the pan. 15 minutes for each side if not too thin. (VVC)

Ragout of Veal or Beef

First of all take a leftover piece of veal roast and chop it finely, then place butter over fire and add one-half tablespoonful of wheat flour, brown this along with the chopped meat, add a little nutmeg to it, a little salt, a little lemon peel, also a bay leaf, a glass of wine or vinegar, and a glass of meat broth; cook this all together in an earthen pot. Let it boil for a quarter or an hour. Serve hot; it is very good. (UC)

Leftover Veal or Beef

So first take the veal [or beef] roast, what's left of it, and chop it fine. Then put butter on the fire and put in 1/2 small spoon of white flour. Cook it with the chopped meat. Add a little mace, a little salt, a little lemon peel, and also a small glass of wine or vinegar, and a small glass of meat broth. Put in an earthenware pot and let it simmer. Cook for a good 1/4 hour. Serve it warm— it is good. (WC)

Mince Meat

4 lbs of apples, 2 lbs of beef (after it is cooked), 3/4 lb of butter and suet, 1 1/4 lbs of sugar, 2 tablespoonsful of cloves, 3 of cinnamon, 1 1/2 of mace, 1 lb of raisins, 1 lb of currants, 3/4 lb of citron, 1 1/2 pint of wine, 1 pt of brandy. Boil the beef soft, then grind apples and beef together. Chop up the raisins, currants, citron, and suet. (VC)

The Way Mother Makes Mince Pie

Boil the meat perfectly done, then run it through a good sausage grinder (or mill), roll your dough and put in a deep plate, then lay your meat on as thick as you wish it, strew a little flour on and then pare and beat two apples very fine and put a layer of these apples, which is enough for one pie, put one spice, and cloves to the taste, then add a little good vinegar, some apple brandy, a little butter, and sugar to sweeten, then put on the top dough and bake half an hour. (UC)

Mock Turtle on Calf's Head

Boil the head until perfectly tender—then take it out, strain the liquor, and set it away until the next day—then skim off the fat, cut up the meat together with the lights, put it in the liquor, put it on the fire and season with salt, pepper, cloves, and mace. Add onion and sweet herbs if you like. Stew it gently for 1/2 an hour. Just before you take it up, add 1/2 pint white wine. [ ] the balls, chop lean veal fine, with a little salt pork add the brains and season with sweet herbs and [ ]. Make it up into balls of the size of half an egg, boil part in the soup and fry the rest and put by themselves. (VVC)

Mutton Chops

Beat and flatten the pieces from the loin and the neck. Season [with] pepper and salt, put in a stew pan with water just sufficient to cover the meat; add vegetables, carrots, pot[atoes]. Send to table with pieces of toasted bread laid around. (VVC)

Mutton and Lamb

Lamb is always roasted. Mutton should be roasted with a brisk fire 1/4 hour before you think it will be done, take off the skin on paper, dredge the meat lightly with flour and baste with butter. A leg requires 2 to 2 1/2 hours, a chin or saddle 1 1/2 to 2 hours, a loin, the same. [Serve with] currant jelly. (VVC)

To Fry Chicken

Cut up the fowl as for fricassee; make some lard very hot in a frying pan, rub each piece over with a mixture of pepper and salt—dip them in flour or crackers (finely rolled) and put in the pan—cover them and fry rather quickly until a fine brown, then turn the other side, leave off the cover and brown nicely—when done take up and add a bit of butter to the pan with a very little hot water and put with chicken. (VVC)

Jellied Chicken

Boil the chicken till tender, chop up, and boil the water down half. Season. Soak 1/2 box gelatin in a little water, add to the froth. Put a thin layer of hard boiled eggs cut in slices, then one of chicken, then gelatin and so on. Prepare this the day before, press somewhat. [Add] 8 or 10 eggs. (VVC)

"Dear Cousins,

...I must give you an account of my last birthday. Wednesday, the 29th of Jan. We were scarcely out of bed, in the morning, when I observed one of my boys come trudging across the fields, behind our house with two chickens in his hands. In joke I said to Augusta, "Well done! I do believe Butcher Beck is sending me a pair of chickens for a birthday present!" And sure enough, for only a few minutes had elapsed, when the boy entered the kitchen with a smiling face and told me that the pair of chickens were sent me as a birthday present by Mr. Beck.

Having put the two creatures into the wood-shed (for want of a more suitable place), I was just about sitting down to breakfast when two boys came upstairs and having congratulated me, handed me a letter containing the request that I would not make any appearances in the schoolroom that morning until 8 o-clock. (The preparation commenced at 7.) As the letter was however written in German and I in a terrible hurry, I laid it aside, intending to decipher it after breakfast, down in the schoolroom. When I made my appearance there, I, to my amazement, found the boys collected around my table, which had been placed in the middle of the room and upon which stood a basket covered with a white cloth. It contained two handsome glass lamps with gild stands, a four-bladed pearl-handle pen knife, several small bottles of ink, etc., together with a paper conveying the best wishes of my boys, followed by a list of their names.

A plate of fresh sausage was presently added to the presents. Having apologized for having disturbed them at their operations, I proceeded to unpack the basket, which afforded the boys much amusement. Before they went home, I treated them to a glass of lemonade and some cakes. They had appointed a Committee, with a president, treasurer, etc., and these collected the contributions and purchased the articles. It was as pleasing as it was unexpected. In the afternoon, we had Cousin Williams, Br. Reichels and Roeppers to vesper and so the day passed very agreeably....

With love to you all, I remain as ever your affectionate cousin,

Henry

Excerpted from a letter from Nazareth, Pennsylvania, dated Feb. 17, 1851, to the Van Vleck daughters, Louisa and Amelia, from their cousin Henry.

Broiled Chicken

Lay the chicken in skimmed milk for about 2 hours. Then put into cold water, cover close and set them over a slow fire and skim well. When done take from the fire and let them remain in water closely covered for 1/2 hour, then drain and serve with white sauce. (VVC)

To Boil Fowl

Dredge them with flour and put in a pot with just enough hot water to cook them; cover closely and put over a moderate fire 15 minutes. As soon as the skim rises, take off and skim. Then cover it again and boil slowly 1/2 hour. Then diminish the fire and let them stew slowly till quite tender. Serve with egg sauce. Stuff or not. Young ones serve with parsley sauce. Boiled fowls should be accompanied with ham or tongue. (VVC)

Roast Pigeons

Stuff with grated bread, butter, parsley, seasoned—dredge—done in 25–30 minutes. Serve with parsley sauce. They may also be fricasseed. Also stewed with ham and peas in the same dish. (VVC)

Pigeon Pie

Put in every one a large piece of butter and the yolk of a hard boiled egg. Paste 1 tablespoon butter to 2 tablespoons flour. Roll rather thick. Lay in the pigeons and on the top some butter rolled in flour. Nearly enough water to fill the dish. Cover and [marinate]. Currant jelly, apples stewed without sugar, dressed celery or any other salad—mashed turnips or squash may be served with roasted birds. (VVC)

Pigeons to Stuff in a Brown Gravy

Lay the pigeons for a few days into vinegar. When you want to cook them, chop a little kidney fat with a little liver add breadcrumbs, a little bit of garlic, onion, a little parsley and sew in the stomach. Thereafter they are browned all over in butter, then pour a glass of wine over, also a glass of vinegar, a bit of strong meat broth or water, a whole onion, bay leaves, a nutmeg; cover it well and let it cook. It will soon be done, then brown a little flour in butter until it becomes dark in color, pour this into the broth and stir, then let it cook along. Cut a few lemon slices into it also. (UC)

School diary of Thomas Schulz (the "second teacher" in the boys school in Salem), Nov. 22, 1817

"I went hunting in the woods and got three squirrels and a rabbit."[11]

Rabbits

Fry some bacon, put the rabbit in the fat with some butter. Turn and cook it till quite white. When it gets [ ] brown, dredge a spoonful of flour over it and when the rabbit is dry lay it on a plate; add another lump of butter; stir it well and when [brown?] add a cupful of water. Put in the rabbit with onions and parsley and the fried bacon, salt, and pepper; let it stew gently over a slow fire for 4 hours. Add the liver and a glass of wine. (VVC)

[Simple Tip for Fish]

All fish should be well cleaned and well done, garnished with horse radish and parsley. (VVC)

To Cook Crayfish Soup

Take raw crayfish, about 1/4 [ ]. Wash them clean and de-vein, etc. Chop them in small pieces. Take a little melted butter in a small pot and let it get right hot. Put the chopped crayfish in and stir gently with a cooking spoon. When they become red, take about a quart or a little less meat broth. Pour it over the crayfish and let it cook for 1/4 hour. After that put it through a cloth or sieve. Press it well out and put it on the fire again. Put mace in, and a little parsley chopped small. Take a roll, cut, and toast it on the grate. Put it in the bowl. Take the sauce from the crayfish; when you have stirred it good, put it over [the roll]. Put it on the chafing dish and then stir in a couple of egg yolks. If you want to, you can also put in some marrow or knobs of butter. Then take it to the table. (WC)

Pickled Salmon

Boil, and after wiping dry, set it to cool; take off the water in which it was boiled and [add] vinegar, each equal parts enough to cover it; add 1 dozen cloves, mace or slice nutmeg, the same quantity, 1 teaspoonful pepper and 1 allspice, and make it boiling hot; skim clean, add a small bit of butter, [ ] and rub over the fish. Sit it in a cool place. When cold it is put for use and will keep long, covered close in a cool place. (VVC)

9

SWEETS

R ITUALS ARE FUNDAMENTAL parts of most cultures. There are
rituals associated with birth, marriage, death, religious cer-
emonies, hunting, cooking, and eating. Food is used to commem-
orate all of life's special occasions, and indeed sometimes an ordinary day becomes special because of a shared meal.

Eating together is what we do to celebrate and to share life.
The influence of food over us can be seen most clearly in the ritual
of mealtime. Superficially, food is the ingredient that keeps us
at the table. On a more substantial level, it is the comfort of the
familiar scents, voices, and words that have made the sharing of
a meal together a precious, sacred time. Sharing a meal strength-
ens families—and each individual within families. The ritual of
mealtime is part of what strengthened Salem Moravians both col-
lectively and individually.

Directions for Baking Pies

The delicacy of pastry depends as much upon the baking as the
making.

* Puff paste requires a quick, even heat—a hot oven will curl
  the paste.

* Tart paste or short requires a degree less heat. (VVC)

Finest Puff Paste—for Puffs/Pies

Heap 1 pound flour into a dish or on the slab—make a hollow in
the center of the flour, break 1 egg into it; then add a teaspoonful
of salt and a piece of butter the size of an egg; mix these lightly
together with a little cold water; add the water, a little at a time,
until the flour is made a nice paste; work it together and roll it
out half an inch thickness; then divide 1 pound butter in 6 parts
spread one over the paste, fold and roll it out again until you can
see the butter—repeat till all the butter is in—roll out 1/4 inch
thick for pies, puffs. The yolk of an egg beaten with a little milk
for gilding. (VVC)

Paste Tart

Roll puff paste to half an inch, cut in cake, the size of a tumbler, bake in a quick oven (1/2 hour) then put jelly, jam, or rich stewed fruit on. (VVC)

Citron Tarts

1 cup sugar
1 tablespoon butter
Whole of 2 eggs
1 tablespoon flour
4 tablespoons milk
1 teaspoon vanilla
For lemon tarts, use the same receipt only add the juice of one lemon. (UC)

* * * * *

"When there were a number of old German people still living in Salem, citron tarts, which are distinctively Salem tarts, were so-called because they were always flavored with lemon and the German word for lemons is 'citronen.'"[12]

* * * * *

[Another for] Citron Tarts

Yellow of six eggs
Butter size of a walnut
Chop the butter with a knife
Lemon drops
1 teacup sugar (UC)

Rice Pie

A wine glass of rice boiled in a quart of milk until soft; take from the fire and having beaten 3 eggs light, stir in gradually add a teaspoon salt and a small teaspoon salt. Line flat pie dish with pie paste and nearly fill. Bake an hour in a quick oven.

Ed. note: The recipe does state "add a teaspoon salt and a small teaspoon salt." (VVC)

Meringue Pie

1 cup of sugar, the yolks of three eggs, 2 1/2 cups of milk, 2 teaspoons of corn starch, the juice and grated peel of one lemon. Beat the yolks lightly, add the sugar, rub the cornstarch in with the

milk, and add that, and then the lemon and beat well together. Line some pans with a rich pastry and fill with the custard and bake. When done take the whites of the three eggs and beat them with a tablespoon of sugar to a stiff froth; spread over the top and brown in the oven. This makes two pies. (VC)

Cream Pies

Bake your crust in a common plate first. Boil one pint of milk, when boiling stir in one half cup of flour, one cup of sugar, and the yolk of two eggs all beaten well together. Cook long enough not to have a [raw] taste. Flavor to your taste. Beat the white to a stiff froth and spread over the pie when filled and brown in the oven. (VC)

Lemon Pie

1/2 pound butter, 1 lb sugar, 6 egg whites and yolks separately, juice of one lemon, grated rind of 2, 1 nutmeg, 1/2 glass brandy, cream the butter and sugar, beat in the yolks, the lemon spices and brandy, stirring in the whites last. (UC)

[Vogler] Lemon Pie

2 tablespoons corn starch dissolved in a little cold water, pour over it 1 teacup boiling water, add 1 cup sugar, 1 egg beat separately, the white put in last, 1 tablespoon butter and flour with a tablespoon lemon extract. (VC)

Spice Cake
Mrs. Hen-

The whites of six eggs, 2 cups of sugar, 3 cups of flour, 1 cup sweet milk, 3/4 cup butter, 2 teaspoons cream of tartar, 1 teaspoon soda, take out 1 cup of the batter, mix in it 1 teaspoon cinnamon, 1/2 nutmeg, and a good deal of chocolate. (UC)

[Vogler] Spice Cake

The whole of 6 eggs, 2 cups of sugar, 3 cups of flour, 1 cup of sweet milk, 3/4 cup of butter, 2 teaspoons cream tartar, 1 teaspoon of soda. Take out a teacup of batter, mix with it one large tablespoon of grated chocolate, 1/2 nutmeg, 1 teaspoon of cinnamon. Fill your mold two inches deep with the white batter, drop in two or three places a spoonful of the dark batter, give to the dark spots a slight stir with the top of the spoon, add more white and proceed as before. (VC)

[Another] Spice Cake

For this cake use the vanilla cake batter, take out about a teacup of batter and mix in it 1 large tablespoonful grated chocolate, 1/2 nutmeg, 1 teaspoon cinnamon, 1/2 allspice. Fill your mould about 2 inches deep with the white batter and drop upon this in two or three places a spoonful of the dark mixture, give it a slight stir with the lip of a teaspoon spreading it on the light batter. Add more of the white and proceed as before. (UC)

Soft Ginger Cake

6 cups flour, 3 molasses, 1 cream, 1 butter, 1 tablespoonful of ginger, 1/2 a spoonful of soda. (UC)

Mrs. Schaffner's Gingercake

1 cup molasses, 1 cup sugar, 2 eggs, 1/2 cup butter, 3 cups flour, 1 teaspoon soda, spice to your taste. (VVC)

Ginger Pound Cake

1/2 pound butter, 1/2 pound sugar, 6 eggs, 1 3/4 pound of flour, 1 teaspoon of cinnamon, 1 teaspoon all spice, 2 tablespoons ginger, 4 teacups of molasses, 1 teaspoon of soda. Beat the sugar and butter to a cream. Whisk the eggs light and add to it, after which put in the spices and molasses and put in the flour and beat all well together. Dissolve the soda in a tablespoon of warm water, and add this last, stirring but little. (VC)

Homeopathic Molasses Cake

Take 6 cups flour, 2 of sugar, 2 of molasses, 1 of milk, 2 teaspoons of saleratus dissolved in the milk, 1/2 lb butter, 4 eggs. Beat the butter and sugar well together then the eggs, add flour and milk and lastly the molasses, fill the pans 3/4 full. Bake 3 hours in moderate heat. (UC)

Vanilla Cake

3 cups sugar, 1 cup butter, 1 cup milk, 4 cups of flour, whites of 15 eggs, 2 teaspoons cream of tartar, 1 teaspoon soda. Bake in jelly cake tins and put together with butter and sugar creamed together very light and flavor with vanilla. (UC)

Fig Cake

This receipt bears a handwritten, penciled "x" and "Tried. Good."

2 cups sugar (dark brown), 1 cup butter, 1 cup water, 1 teaspoon
each of cloves, cinnamon, and nutmeg, 4 eggs, 2 cups chopped
raisins, one-half glass wine, 1 lb. figs, 2 cups currants, 3 cups
flour, and 2 teaspoons baking powder. Alternate with 2 cups sugar,
three-fourths cup butter, 1 cup sweet milk, 1 cup cornstarch, 2
cups flour, 3 teaspoons baking powder, and whites 6 eggs. (VVC)

A Cherry Cake

Take a roll and cook it in milk until it is thick. When it is cold,
take 1/2 cup fresh butter and let it melt. Stir it with 6 eggs to a
foam. Add some grated lemon peel, sugar, and ground cinnamon,
and some ripe cherries in season. Stir all together with the roll
cooked in milk and put in a greased casserole and bake. (WC)

Orange Cake

Make the dough of any receipt you wish. For four layers it takes
the white of one egg beat to a froth, then grate an orange, peeling
and all, be sure to let all the juice go in then pick out the little
pieces of pulp that did not grate and make it thick enough with
sugar. (VC)

Lemon Cake

2 cups sugar, 1 cup milk, 1 cup butter, 4 cups of flour, 5 eggs, 1
teaspoon soda, 2 of cream of tartar, 2 ounces of citron, ice and
cut in small pieces. Bake thin in pans. (UC)

* * * * *

*Sisters could depend on the Single Brothers to make important bak-
ing items such as tin kitchenware, cake pans, and cookie cutters.*

* * * * *

Cocoanut Cake

1 1/2 cup of sugar, 1/2 cup butter, whites of 3 eggs, 1 cup milk,
3 cups flour, 1/2 teaspoon soda, 1 cream tartar, grated cocoanut
leaving half a teacup to sprinkle over the top, either before baking or just after icing as preferred. (VC)

[Vogler] Cocoanut Cake

4 cups flour, 3 cups sugar, 1 cup butter, 1 cup sweet milk, 6 eggs, 1 teaspoon soda and 2 cream of tartar.

Iceing:
The white of three eggs, 1 lb sugar, and one cocoanut. Bake in flat pans. (VC)

Fruit Cake

From Mrs. Meinung.

Rub 6 oz butter with 1/2 lb white sugar, add the beaten yolks of 6 eggs, 1/2 lb flour, mace enough to flavor well, the beaten whites of 6 eggs, stir it well, then another 1/2 lb of flour, 1 wine glass of wine, and 1 of brandy. Mix well. Chop 2 lbs seedless raisins, rub them and 1/4 lb of citron (cut in slips) in flour, then add to the dough and bake in a moderate oven. If you have prepared orange or lemon peel, add them with the syrup. (UC)

Nut Cake

2 cups of sugar, 1 cup of butter, 3 cups of flour, 1 cup of cold water, 4 eggs, 1 teaspoon soda, 2 of cream tartar, 2 cupfuls kernels of hickory nuts or walnuts picked out and added last. (VC)

Neapolitan Cake Black

1/2 cup molasses, 1/2 cup strong coffee, 1/2 cup butter, 1 cup brown sugar, 2 1/4 cups sifted flour, 2 eggs, 1 teaspoon soda, 1/2 of mace, 1 of cloves, 1 of cinnamon, 1/2 lb raisins, 1/2 lb currants, 1/2 lb citron.

Paste chocolate: whites of 3 eggs, 1 1/2 cups sugar, 3 tablespoons chocolate, 1 teaspoon vanilla. (UC)

Tri-Color Cake

1 cup white sugar, 1/2 cup butter, 1/2 cup sweet milk, whites of 5 eggs, 1 1/2 cup flour, 1/2 teaspoon soda, 1 of cream of tartar, flavor with orange. Bake in two tins as quickly as possible.

For the pink cake: Take just half of the above using red sugar sand and flavor with the juice and rind of half a lemon. Bake in one pan.

For the yellow cake: Take the yolks of 5 eggs, light brown sugar, the same proportions as the white cake, add 1/2 lb chopped citron. Bake in two tins. (UC)

Chocolate Cake

2 cups of sugar, 1 cup butter, yolks of 3 eggs, whites of 2, 1 cup of milk, 3 1/2 cups of flour, 1/2 teaspoon soda, 1 of cream tartar. (VC)

Icing with Chocolate

Whites of 3 eggs, 1 1/2 cups sugar, 3 tablespoons grated cocoa, 1 teaspoon vanilla (VC)

Ed. note: Later in the original receipt book, this recipe reappears, with this alteration: "yolks of 5 eggs" instead of 3 egg whites.

Cream Cake

1 large coffee cup of sugar
1 tablespoonful of butter
2 eggs
1 cup of sour milk
1 teaspoon of soda
1 pt of flour and a little nutmeg. Bake in pie pans. It will make two. (VC)

[Van Vleck] Cream Cake

"Excellent with rich cream."

Four cups of flour; three cups of sugar; two cups of butter; one cup of cream; five eggs; one teaspoonful of essence of lemon; and one teaspoonful of saleratus, dissolved in a little milk; beat it well and bake it in a quick oven. (VVC)

Snow Cake

This is from Prize Recipes. *A date of 1881 peeps out from behind pasted clippings on top of this printed book. This recipe has a penciled "x" by it and "try this."*

Three-fourths cup butter, 2 cups sugar, 1 cup milk, 1 cup cornstarch, 2 cups flour, 1 and one-half teaspoonsful baking powder. Mix cornstarch, flour, and baking powder together, add butter and sugar alternately with the milk. Lastly add the whites of 7 eggs. Flavor to taste. Never fails to be good. (VVC)

Washington Cake

1 lb of sugar, 1 lb of flour, 1/2 lb of butter, 6 eggs, 1 teacup of milk, wine glass of brandy, 1 teaspoon of soda, and two of cream of tartar. (VC)

What do you prepare for the President? Certainly, the Sisters took great care in providing special, delicious meals to George Washington when he visited Salem in the spring of 1791. President Washington stayed at the Salem Tavern.

* * * * *

Carolina Cake

2 cups of flour, 2 of sugar, 1 of sweet milk, whites of 5 eggs, 3 tablespoons of butter, 1/4 teaspoon full of soda, 1/2 of cream of tartar. (UC)

Rice Cake

1 cup butter
1 pound sugar
4 eggs
1 cup of milk
3 cups flour (2 of rice flour; 1 of wheat)
2 heaping teaspoonsful of Royal baking powder
Rose water if liked. (VVC)

Strong Cake

9 eggs, the weight of 9 [eggs] in sugar and 6 in flour. It is not to be stirred after the flour is in. (VC)

Economy Cake

1 cup butter, 2 cups sugar, 1 cup milk, 1 cup chopped raisins, 2 eggs, 1 tablespoonful soda, spice to taste with cloves, nutmeg, and cinnamon. 3 cups flour. (UC)

Field Cake

1 cup of sugar, 1 cup lard, 1 teaspoon of salt mixed with the flour, 1 quart of buttermilk, 1 tablespoon of soda, 2 eggs, cinnamon to taste. (UC)

Drop Cake

1 cup of sugar, 1/2 cup of butter, 1/2 cup of water, 2 cups of flour, 1 teaspoon soda, 2 teaspoons of ginger; if you use molasses, beat well together and bake quick. (UC)

A Good Family Cake

Take rice and wheat flour, of each 6 ounces, the yolks and whites of 9 eggs, 1/2 pound of lump sugar pounded and sifted, and 1/2 ounce of carraway seeds. Having beaten this one hour, bake it for the same time in a quick oven. This is a very light cake and is very proper for young people and delicate stomachs. (VVC)

Rail Road Cake

1 cup of milk, 3 of flour, 2 of sugar, 1/2 of butter, 8 eggs, 2 teaspoons full of cream of tartar, rubbed through the sieve with the flour, a teaspoonful of soda, flavor to your taste. (UC)

Ed. note: This recipe is identical to the following one from the Van Vleck family with the exception of eggs. The additional eggs that this recipe calls for give the cake a richer taste and help hold it together. Such variations can be found in other recipes among the different collections—just another glimpse of how cooks have always modified recipes to suit their tastes.

Railroad Cake

This receipt, as several others reproduced throughout this book, was originally written on a tiny scrap of paper. No doubt, it was asked or received from a friend or neighbor either after partaking of a delightful dish or hearing good reviews of one.

1 cup of milk, 3 of flour, 2 of sugar, 1/2 cup butter, 3 eggs, 2 teaspoons cream of tartar sifted through the sieve with the flour, 1 teaspoonful of soda stirred with the milk. Flavor. (VVC)

White Mountain Cake

1 lb of flour, 1 lb of sugar, 1/2 of butter, 6 eggs, 1 cup sweet milk, 1 small teaspoon soda, put in the milk, 2 teaspoons cream of tartar. Bake in pie tin then put together with icing. (UC)

[Vogler] White Mountain Cake

1 lb of sugar, 1 lb of flour, 1/2 lb butter, 4 eggs, 1 cup sweet milk, 1 teaspoon soda, 2 of cream tartar. (VC)

Poor People's Pound Cake

2 cups of bread dough, 1 cup of white sugar, 3 eggs well beaten, 1 teaspoonful of soda, dissolved in a little milk, 1/2 cup of butter, flavor to your taste. (UC)

Western Pound Cake

1 lb sugar, 5 eggs, 5 ounces butter, 4 cups of flour, 1 teaspoon of soda, 2 of cream of tartar, 1 teacup of milk. Dissolve the soda in the milk, the cream of tartar to be rubbed through the sieve with the flour, the butter, sugar, and yolks of egg to be stirred together well, the whites to be beaten to a froth by degrees; add the flour and milk, and lastly the white and the eggs. Flavor with whatever you like. (UC)

Pound Cake

Take 3/4 lb. butter, beat it in an earthen pan with your hand, one way, till it is like a fine thick cream; then have ready 10 eggs, with half the whites beat them well first, and also beat them up with the butter, working into it a pound and 1/4 flour, a pound and 1/4 sugar and a few carraways for an hour with your hand or a wooden spoon. Butter a pan, put it in, and then bake it an hour in a quick oven. (VVC)

Lady Cake

1 cup sugar, 1 cup butter, 1 cup milk, whites of 6 eggs, 3 cups flour, 1/2 teaspoon soda, 1 teaspoon cream of tartar. (UC)

[Vogler] Lady Cake

1 lb of sugar, ten ounces of butter, 1 lb of flour, white of 16 eggs, 3 oz of almonds, 1 teaspoonful of yeast powder. (VC)

French Cake

2 cups sugar, 1/2 of butter, 1 cup of milk, 3 cups of flour, 3 eggs, 1 teaspoon of soda, 2 cream of tartar. (VC)

Muffin Cake

6 eggs, 1 pint milk, butter the size of a walnut, make as thick as flannel cake batter. (UC)

Silver Cake

1 lb sugar, 3/4 lb flour, 1/2 lb butter, white of 14 eggs, 1 teaspoon soda, and 2 cream of tartar. (VC)

[Vogler] Silver Cake

The whites of 8 eggs, 2 cups sugar, 2 1/2 cups flour, 1/2 cup butter, 1/2 cup sour cream, 1/2 teaspoon soda, one cream of tartar. (VC)

[Salem] Silver Cake

1 pound sugar, 3/4 pound flour, 6 ounces butter, the whites of 14 eggs, and essence of lemon. Stir the butter to foam and then add the sugar, then the eggs, add a teaspoon of soda dissolved in milk, and a little cream of tartar, and be sure to add a little flour lastly. (UC)

[Another] Silver Cake

Mix together 2 teacupsful of white sugar and a half teacup of butter, then add the whites of 4 eggs, beat to a stiff froth; add to this 1 teacup full of cold water and after it is well combined stir in 3 cupsful of sifted flour, into which a measure each of acid and soda has been stirred and sifted, and stir briskly for 2 minutes. Bake quickly. (UC)

Gold Cake

Make like Silver cake and use the yolks of 4 eggs instead of mixing the sugar and butter together first, [beat] up the yolks, then add the sugar and stir it well, next the butter and so on. (UC)

[Vogler] Gold Cake

1 lb of flour, 1 lb of sugar, 3/4 lb butter, yolks of 14 eggs, 1 cup of milk, 1 teaspoon soda, and 2 cream of tartar. (VC)

Marble Cake

2 cups of sugar, 1 of butter, 1 of cream, 4 of flour, a little soda, whites of 7 eggs and yolks of 7 eggs, 1 cup butter, 1 of sugar, 1 of molasses, 1 of cream, a little soda, 5 cups flour. (UC)

Jenny Lind Cake

2 cups flour, 1 1/2 cups sugar, 1/2 cup butter, 3 eggs, 1/2 cup milk, 1/2 teaspoon soda, and one of cream tartar. (VC)

Jenny Lind

2 cups flour, 1 1/2 cups sugar, 1/2 cup butter, 3 eggs, 1/2 cup sweet milk, 1/2 teaspoon of soda, and a little salt, 1 teaspoon cream tartar. (UC)

Composition Cake

1 pound flour, 1 lb sugar, 1/2 pound butter, 7 eggs, 1/2 pint of cream, and 1 gill of brandy. (UC)

["Good"] Delicate Cake

"good"

3 cups of flour, 2 cups of sugar, 3/4 of a cup of sweet milk, 1/2 cup of butter, white of 6 eggs, 1/2 teaspoon of soda, and one of cream of tartar. (VC)

Delicate Cake

Nearly three cups of flour, two cups of sugar, three-fourths of a cup of sweet milk, the whites of six eggs, one teaspoonfull of cream of tartar, half a teaspoon full of soda, half a cup of butter. Flavor with lemon. (UC)

["The Best"] Delicate Cake

This recipe has penciled in beside the inked writing, "the best."

The white of 12 eggs, 12 oz sugar, 12 oz flour, 9 oz butter, 1 teaspoon soda, 2 cream tartar. (VC)

[Vogler] Delicate Cake

1 1/2 cups sugar, 1/2 cup butter, whites of 4 eggs, 3 cups flour, 1/2 cup milk, 1 teaspoon cream tartar, 1/2 teaspoon of soda. (VC)

White Cake

3 cups sifted flour, 1 1/2 cups sugar, 1 cup sweet milk, 1 egg, 2 tablespoonfuls of butter, 2 teaspoonsful cream tartar, 1 teaspoonful essence lemon, 1 teaspoonful soda. Beat the butter and sugar to a cream, then add the milk (in which the soda should be dissolved), the egg well beaten, and the essence. Mix with the above 2 cups flour, then, lastly, add the last cup of flour in which the cream tartar has been stirred. Bake in pans or basins in a quick oven. It will make a very nice cake indeed. (UC)

Brides Cake

1 lb of sugar, 1 lb of flour, 3/4 lb of butter, the white of 12 eggs, 1 teaspoon of soda, and two cream of tartar. (VC)

Heart Cake

1/2 pound sugar, 6 eggs, 1/2 teaspoon of saleratus. Shorten well with butter. (UC)

Mrs. Eng's Cake

3 cups sugar, 2 cups butter, 6 eggs, 6 cups of flour, 1 cup sour milk, 1 teaspoon of saleratus, 1 glass wine, 1 brandy, 2 pounds raisins or currants, nutmeg, [ ]. (VVC)

Cake—Sponge

This is another receipt from Prize Recipes. *A date of 1881 peeps out from behind pasted clippings on top of the printed book. She penciled an "x" by it.*

Whites of 10 eggs, 1 and one-half tumblers sugar, 1 tumbler flour, 1 teaspoon salt, 1 small teaspoonful creamtarter, 1 teaspoonful flavoring. Bake one-half hour in a quick oven. (VVC)

Sponge Cake

Take 6 eggs, 2 cups of sugar, 2 cups of flour, 2 large tablespoonsful of cold water, and a little lemon juice if you like. Beat whites and yolks of eggs separately; beat the sugar into the yolks, then the flour, next the water, and the whites last. Bake in a moderate oven. Also 1 teaspoonful of soda and 2 of cream of tartar. (UC)

[Vogler] Sponge Cake

12 eggs, the weight of eggs in sugar, 1/2 their weight in flour, lemon to flavor. Beat the yolks and whites very light, the sugar with the yolks, when they are stiff and smooth add the flavor, then the flour, lastly the whites beaten very lightly. (VC)

Tea Cake

1 tea cup of butter, 1 of milk, 2 of sugar, 3 of flour, 4 eggs, and some saleratus. Bake in a pan. (UC)

Cupcakes

To 5 cups flour take 3 cups sugar, 5 eggs, 1 cup milk, 1 cup melted butter, 1 teaspoon full pearl ash, 1 stem glass full rum, spice to your taste. Raisins are a great addition. (VVC)

Cup Cake

One cup butter, 2 cups of sugar, 1 cup of milk, 4 cups flour, 4 eggs, 1 teaspoon saleratus. (UC)

White Cupcake

1 cup sour milk, 1 of butter, 2 of powdered sugar, 4 of sifted flour. Stir the butter and sugar together until quite light by degrees, add the cream alternately with half the flour. Add a large teaspoonful cinnamon with 8 drops of oil of lemon. Lastly stir in a very small teaspoonful of saleratus. Having stirred _well_ fill it into little tins, set them in a moderate oven, bake them about 20 minutes. (VVC)

Vanilla Cup Cake

3/4 cup butter
3/4 cup [sour?] milk
1 1/2 cups sugar
2 cups of flour
3 eggs
3/4 teaspoon soda
same of cream of tartar
vanilla (VVC)

New York Cup Cake

4 eggs, 3 cups sugar, 4 of flour, 1 of butter, 1 of milk, small teaspoonful of soda, some nutmeg. (UC)

Molasses Cupcake
"Delicious!"

2 cups molasses, 2 butter, 1 milk, 1 teaspoon powdered saleratus in hot water, nutmeg, and 2 well beaten eggs. Stir in by degrees enough flour to make it as stiff as you can stir easily with a spoon, beat it well until it is very light, rub a 2 [pan] over with a bit of butter—line with white paper and put the cake in. Bake 20 minutes in a quick oven. Fry with a brown [splint?] at the thickest part. (VVC)

Ginger Cakes

1 gal. of molasses, 8 teacups of sugar, 16 tablespoons of ginger, 3 quarts of melted lard, 8 tablespoons of soda dissolved in 6 teacups of boiling water. Add flour enough to roll and cut into shapes. (VC)

Cousin Emma's Ginger Cakes

"I used this receipt in 1891."

To 3 quarts of molasses take 1/2 lb of sugar
1/2 lb lard or butter
1/4 cup cloves
Tablespoon of soda dissolved in boiling water
1 ounce ginger
1 1/2 of cinnamon
3/4 ounce cloves
Flour stiff enough to roll out (VC)

Ginger Nuts

1 1/2 lbs sugar, 6 eggs, white beaten to a froth, stir the yolks and sugar together, 2 teaspoons soda, 2 tablespoons ginger, cinnamon and cloves, flour to make a stiff batter; let it stand half an hour to rise, then work in flour so you can roll out; dissolve the soda in a little warm water. (UC)

[Vogler] Ginger Nuts

To 1 1/2 lbs of brown sugar mix the yolks of six eggs, before putting in the yolks mix 3 teaspoonfuls of soda dry with the sugar. 2 teaspoonfuls of ground ginger, 2 of cloves. Froth the white of the eggs and add it. After stirring it well add enough flour to make it about as stiff as loaf cake when you pour it into the mould. Then let it stand about 1/2 an hour; add enough flour to roll it out. (VC)

Ginger Snaps

1 large cup of butter and lard mixed, 1 coffee cup of sugar, 1 cup molasses, 1/2 cup water, 1 tablespoon of ginger, 1 of cinnamon, 1 of cloves, 1 teaspoon soda dissolved in a hot water, flour for pretty stiff dough. Roll out thin and bake quickly. (VC)

Gingerbread or Gingerbread Kisses

1 pound flour, 1/2 pound sugar, 1/4 butter, 6 eggs to a cup of ginger.

To makes kisses:
Take the white of 4 eggs to 3/4 pound of lump or loaf sugar, fine pulverized, then take a large bowl, have it quite dry, without sugar you beat the white of 4 eggs till it gets like snow, with a silver spoon and when the spoon stands quite upright in the snow, it will be good: now you add the fine pulverized sugar to it, and with a large iron spoon beat this well again and when well mixed then you put 2 teaspoonfulls of good vinegar in it; beat all together so long till you can pour it from a teaspoon stiff, set it near one another on paper. (VVC)

Molasses Cakes

"very good"

To 2 quarts of molasses, 2 lbs of sugar, 1 1/2 pt of lard or butter melted, 1 tablespoon of soda, 1 ounce ginger, 1 1/2 ounces cinnamon and mace (each), cloves only half the quantity. (VC)

Molasses Cookies

3 cups of molasses, 2 eggs, 1 3/4 cups lard (it is not necessary to take that much). 3 large teaspoonfuls of soda dissolved in boiling water, 2 teaspoons of ginger. Flour enough to roll out, not too stiff. 1 cup of sugar or not as you like. (VC)

(Christmas) Sugar Cakes

2 pounds flour, 1 pound sugar, 1 pound butter, 1 nutmeg, 1 tablespoonful cinnamon, 1 teaspoon saleratus, rose water, 6 eggs, 1/2 gill milk, mix with a spoon as quick as possible. (VVC)

Mrs. Butner's Christmas Cakes

2 quarts molasses, 2 pounds sugar, 1 good pint melted lard, 1/4 teacup of cloves, same of ginger and of cinnamon, 1 good teaspoonful of soda. (VVC)

Good Christmas Cakes

4 qts molasses, 2 lb sugar, 1 qt lard, 3/4 cup cinnamon, 1/2 cup ginger, 1/2 cup cloves, tablespoon soda. (VC)

Salem Christmas Cakes

1 gallon of molasses
2 lbs sugar
2 lbs lard
2 small tablespoons of soda
Scalded milk about 1/2 a cup of boiling water
a small cup of cloves
a small cup of ginger—and any other spices to suit the taste (VVC)

Christmas Cakes

To 1 gallon molasses take 2 1/2 pounds of sugar, 4 ounces soda,
2 1/2 pounds lard, 8 tablespoons ginger, cinnamon, 4 cloves.

*Ed. note: Before some later revision, this receipt first listed 3 pounds
sugar, 3 ounces soda, 3 pounds lard; it included 1 dozen eggs, and
"flour to make it just so it can be worked."* (UC)

THE MORAVIAN STAR

WHAT STARTED AS A lesson in geometry in Germany's Moravian
boarding schools around the 1850s became a worldwide symbol
proclaiming the hope of Christmas.[13] No longer only adorning
Moravian homes, the large, lighted, multi-pointed star makes an
annual appearance on many porches, in hallways, and churches.
The first star had alternating points of red and white. Now all-
white stars dominant Advent. Displaying the star is more than
a Christmastime ritual; it acts as a visual reminder that Christ,
our Savior, was born in a stable on that long-ago night. *"May we
continue to seek our Savior."*

Jackson Cakes

5 eggs, 2 teacups of sugar, 1 of lard or butter, 1 teaspoon of soda,
2 of cream of tartar, flour stiff enough to roll out. Flavor to taste.
Dissolve the soda in a little sweet milk. (VC)

Such Cakes

3 eggs, 1 cup sugar, 1 cup buttermilk, 1/2 cup lard, 1/2 teaspoon
soda rubbed through the sieve, also a little salt. (UC)

Rice Cakes

Maria's receipt.

2 tablespoonsful less than 1 pound of rice flour
1 pound of white sugar
1/2 pound of butter
10 eggs
The whites of the eggs in last. Bake one hour. Very good. (VVC)

Fast-Night Cakes

1 qt of milk, 1 pint ribbles to a rising, then about 3 oz butter (or lard), sugar enough to sweeten it, 5 eggs, and a little cinnamon, the dough tolerable stiff, then roll it out as you please; some can be baked with dried fruit or preserves in them. (UC)

Little While Cakes

Dry half a pound flour, rub into it a very little pounded sugar, one ounce of butter, one egg, a few [ ]. Bake 15 minutes on tin plates. (VVC)

Flannel Cakes

2 eggs, 1 teaspoon soda, a little pinch of sugar and salt, buttermilk, flour to make a tolerable stiff batter, beat all together and stir into the flour. (UC)

Shrewsbury Cakes

Take 6 ounces butter, 1 lb or more flour, mix it well then add 3/4 pound sugar, 4 eggs, and 1 teaspoonful pearl or pot ash. (VVC)

White Cakes

1 lb sugar, 4 eggs, 1/2 lb butter, a little soda just enough flour to roll out, nothing warm, and work as little as possible. Mix butter and flour together and the sugar and eggs together. (UC)

[Vogler] White Cakes

1 lb of sugar, 1/2 lb of butter, 4 eggs, 1/3 teaspoon of soda, flour stiff enough to roll out. Flavor to taste. (VC)

Jumbles, Plain

Take 6 eggs, 2 or 3 spoonfuls of Damask rose water, beat them together; put in a pound of loaf sugar, beaten and sifted, mix them well together and put in as much fine flour dried as will make them roll out, which you must do, then tie and lay them in what fashion you please; bake them on paper tins or plates and be sure to take them off as soon as they come out of the oven. (butter) (VVC)

Tea Cakes

2 cups of sugar, two eggs, 1 cup of butter, 1 cup of sour milk, 1 teaspoon of soda, thicken with flour, roll, [cut], and bake. Flavor to taste. (VC)

Delicious Tea-Cakes

Beat to a cream two cupfuls of sugar, a cupful of butter and an egg, add a cupful of milk and stir it well through the other ingredients; grate in a little nutmeg. Sift into a bowl three cupfuls of flour, or a little more if necessary to make the dough stiff enough to roll out, with two heaping teaspoonfuls of baking powder; then add the flour to the other mixture, a little at a time, stirring briskly to keep the flour from lumping up. When the flour is all in, if the dough is stiff enough to roll out dust the pastry board well with flour, turn the dough out of the bowl and roll it out very thin. Cut out in little shapes with a cutter, lay them on well-greased baking tins and bake in a quick oven. While the cakes are hot sprinkle the top of them with sugar. (VVC)

Cookies

6 eggs whites and yolks separately, 1 cup of butter, 3 cups sugar, flour to make just stiff enough to be moulded with well floured hands. Flavor with lemon. Make in round cakes and bake quick. (VC)

[Van Vleck] Cookies

Take 1 cup of butter and 4 cups of flour, [mix] them well together. 1 cup of white sugar, 2 eggs, beat them to a froth. Add 1/2 teaspoon of soda and 1/4 teaspoon of cinnamon. Mix together, roll thin. Bake in a moderate oven. (VVC)

Wafers

Take 1 pound flour, 1/4 lb butter, 2 eggs beat, 1 glass wine, and nutmeg. Bake on papers. (UC)

[Vogler] Wafers

8 eggs, 1 lb sugar, 1 lb flour, 1 teacup of butter. This will make 30 wafers. (VC)

Sponge Drops

3 eggs—beat the whites to a stiff froth—add yolks, one cup of sugar, and one heaping coffee cup of flour into whites, a teaspoon of cream of tartar and 1/2 teaspoon soda are thoroughly mixed— flavor with lemon—and drop with a teaspoon on buttered tins— bake. "Household." (UC)

Drop Sponge Cake or Lady Fingers

1/2 pound powdered sugar, 1/2 lb flour, four egg yolks and whites separate, beaten very stiff, 1 lemon, all the juice and half the grated rind. Drop on buttered paper, not too near together. Try one and if it runs, beat the mixture some minutes longer, adding a very little flour. Bake in a quick oven. (VC)

Stritz or Funnel Cakes

1 pint <u>half</u> of flour, 1/2 of sweet milk. A lump of butter size of a walnut or larger. If you have it plenty, make the milk hot, put the butter in when you put the milk on the stove, when melted and the milk is hot but not boiling, pour it over the flour and mix well, put a little soda dry in the flour before you add the milk, then add three eggs, and stir well. Fry in hot lard. Let the batter run through a funnel. (VC)

Strumbendels

2 cups sugar, 1 cup butter, 1 cup milk, 4 eggs, 1 teaspoon saler- atus, and a little cinnamon. (UC)

Strumbendlles

3/4 of a pound of butter, 1 lb of sugar, 9 eggs, 1/2 teacup full of spirits (mix the butter and flour together) and (the sugar and eggs together). 1 teaspoon soda. This kind we make. (UC)

Ed note: The teaspoon of soda was added later, noting that "this kind we make." The amount of flour isn't stated, so we don't know how much is recommended.

Crullers

1/2 pint sweet milk, 1/2 cup sugar, 1/2 cup butter or lard, 3 eggs, a little soda (less than a teaspoon), 1/2 teaspoon salt, flour enough to make a smooth dough. Flavor to taste. (VC)

Crollers

1 cup sugar, 1/2 cup milk, whites of 4 eggs, 1/2 cup butter, then stiffen with flour, 1 teaspoon soda, 2 of cream tartar. (UC)

[Another Recipe for] Crollers

Beat 12 eggs well then add 1 pound sugar, 1/2 lb butter, flour till it is stiff enough to roll out. Bake in lard. (UC)

Bitter Macaroons

One takes about 1 [pound] bitter and 1/4 [pound] sweet almonds, 2 1/2 [pounds] sugar and the whites from about 20 eggs and proceeds exactly as [given on page 81 Winkler's Notes on Preparing Macaroons]. One takes care to give the bitter macaroons a round form. (WC)

* * * * *

As can be noticed by the abundance of dessert-type recipes, the Salem Moravians enjoyed sweet dishes. One reason other cooking categories are not as hefty isn't due to lack of making other dishes; instead, it may be because the Sisters regarded diet staples (such as vegetable dishes that everyone would regularly fix) in such a manner that would not have rendered them necessary to commit to paper.

* * * * *

Macaroons

Take a pound of almonds, let them be scalded, blanched, and thrown into cold water, then dry them in a cloth and pound them into a mortar; moisten them with orange flower water or the white of an egg, less they turn to an oil; after this take an equal quantity or fine powdered sugar with 3 or 4 beaten whites of eggs; beat all well together and shape (with your hands dipped in cold water) them on paper with a spoon. Bake them on plates in a gentle oven 3/4 of an hour. (VVC)

Sweet Macaroons

* One scalds 1 pound of sweet almonds in boiling water, then pours them out into cold water, in which they stay for only a couple of minutes. One skins them and washes them and then lets them dry under a napkin for 24 hours.

* From these almonds, one takes a handful and puts them into a stone mortar or into a grinding bowl and crushes them fine, but not so fine that they release their oil. On the crushed mass one pours the white of one egg, stirs and mixes it until well incorporated so that it becomes a fine dough.

* One now empties the mortar and proceeds with the remaining almonds in the same way. If one egg white is not sufficient, then one must take more. This cannot be determined exactly, since eggs are not all the same size and contain more or less white.

* When the almond mass is thoroughly worked up, then one pours it into the mortar again, or into a grinding bowl, and add 2 [tablespoons] of very finely pulverized sugar along with the grated peel of two lemons.

* One stirs it all until it is well incorporated and pours enough egg white into it so that the dough has the necessary consistency. To 1 [pound] of almonds one needs usually only 12 to 18 parts of egg.

* When the dough is prepared, then one takes a ruler made from hard wood, two fingers in width, and provided with a handle. One lays some dough on this, takes it with the left hand...and puts it with a clean knife on an oval sheet of paper in little mounds about a finger thick, which must set 1 1/2 inches apart from one another.

* When this work is completed one puts the macaroons on a metal sheet into a moderately hot oven and lets them bake slowly for 3/4 hour. (WC)

Chocolate Macaroons

When the sweet macaroon dough is ready according to the above recipe, one lays 1/4 pound chocolate on a metal sheet and lets it soften over a charcoal fire, then puts it on a plate and adds about 2 spoonfuls of the almond dough to it. After the mixture is well stirred together one places it in the mortar and into the remaining dough pours one spoonful of very finely ground cinnamon or a teaspoon full of vanilla or both if one pleases and works everything properly through. In baking, great care is required. (WC)

[Winkler's Notes on Preparing Macaroons]

The preparation of macaroons requires much care and precision. One should see particularly:

1. That the almonds are thoroughly dry before one pours them into the mortar.
2. One should be careful in breaking the eggs. There must not be <u>one</u> drop of yellow in the whites. Otherwise the whole mass of dough would be ruined and the macaroons would fall in the oven instead of rising, become unsightly, and lose in weight.
3. The oven must be heated only moderately. Almonds and sugar burn easily. If one does not exercise the proper caution here, the surface of the macaroons will burn while the inside will remain raw. In order to proceed completely surely one puts a couple in the oven as a test and lets them bake 3/4 hour. If then they are not burnt but of a pretty golden color, the oven has the appropriate degree of heat; if, on the other hand, they are black on the bottom, that is an indication that the heat underneath is higher than that on the top, and in this case one must lay two or three sheets of paper on the metal sheet to moderate the effect of this. Only after one has tested the temperature of the oven by this means does one bring the macaroon dough onto the paper, and only when they are fully cooled does one remove the macaroons from the paper. (WC)

Filled Macaroons

Sweet macaroon dough (see above) is placed on round wafer sheets. By means of a little round stick a finger thick one puts a small indentation on each macaroon and lets them bake as described above. Then one fills the hollowed out part with raspberry, cherry, or other jelly. One does not lift this pastry off the paper, but rather cuts the paper around each macaroon. (WC)

Filled Macaroon Torte

One takes the wafer cut to fit the vessel, lays it on a piece of paper and spreads it, as thick as the back of a knife, with sweet macaroon dough, then surrounds the rim with oval macaroons, which rest on the tapered end. On this, more rich macaroons are laid in a latticework pattern and after this the torte is placed in the oven. After 3/4 hour one takes it out and fills the spaces copiously with all sorts of fruit rolled in sugar, such as cherries, raspberries, yellow plums, and the like. (WC)

Spice Macaroons

To the sweet macaroon dough one adds a spoonful of finely ground cinnamon, 6 to 8 finely ground cloves, a spoonful of finely chopped Seville orange peel, a spoonful of finely chopped candied lemon along with the grated peel of 2 lemons. All these ingredients are thoroughly stirred into the almond dough and prepared in oval or round forms. (WC)

Spice Macaroon Torte

One sticks together as many wafer sheets as are required for the size of the cake. Place the basin which is to be used for the preparation of the same onto the wafer sheets and cut them accordingly. Now one covers it a finger thick with the above described spice macaroon dough and puts it in the oven. While the torte bakes one puts some sugar (about 8 to 12 lot [1 lot =10 grams]) in a pan and cooks it in orange blossom water until it makes high bubbles when stirred with the skimming ladle. When the torte is baked light brown one pours the sugar mixture over it and puts it back in the oven for a few minutes to dry the icing. These tortes are rich in aroma and flavor. (WC)

Yellow Almond Pastry

We have seen that in macaroons and macaroon tortes one can use only the white of the egg. However, when at certain times of year eggs are expensive, one must seek to use the yolks in some way. We recommend yellow almond pastry for this purpose.

According to whether one has much or little of the yolks in stock, one takes 1 or 2 [pounds] of sweet almonds, scalds and shells them, washes them, and lets them dry well. Then one pulverizes them well in a mortar or grinding bowl along with the egg yolks into a very fine fairly stiff dough.

One adds to each pound of almonds a pound of finely granulated sugar and the grated peels of 2 lemons, kneads the dough thoroughly on a table sprinkled with sugar and forms from it as one will all sorts of small shapes, such as: small loaves, round or cube shaped, small pretzels, clover leaves, and the like.

One places the pastry on a metal pan lined with paper and puts it in a moderately hot oven, and takes it out when it has baked to a bright gold [color]. One covers these pastries with the icing described above for macaroon torte. When it has cooled thoroughly, one carefully removes it from the paper. (WC)

Almond Rolls

With two stale milk rolls take 1/4 lb finely ground almonds, as fine as for almond tarts, take 1/4 lb sugar, 1 tsp cinnamon powder, a little rose water, take a little bread crumbs which are softened in sweet milk, a little bit of small raisins. Take the dry rolls and grate them on a grater all around. Take out the inside so you can fill them, then brown them in butterfat good and brown. Thereafter, place them in a bowl, pour over almonds, sugar and cinnamon, cut the almonds up finely. Take 1/2 pint wine, cook it in a saucepan. Take a little sugar, small raisins, and a little lemon peel finely cut up and cook some more after boil. Pour it in the bowl with the rolls, but not on top, so they do not get soft, then serve. (UC)

For Nut Candy

While making into balls mold an almond meal in the center of each ball and roll in coarse sugar and you have nice cream almonds. A mold the half of an English walnut into the soft sugar and you have Cream Walnuts. (VC)

Chocolate Caramels

1/4 lb chocolate, 2 lbs brown sugar, butter size of an egg, 2 tablespoons vinegar, 1/2 teacup sweet milk. let it cook 15 minutes and then try it by dropping a little into cold water. When it hardens it is done. Pour into buttered pans. Stir as little as possible. (UC)

Chocolate Drops

2 1/2 cups of pulverized or granulated sugar
1/2 cup of cold water
Boil 4 minutes, place in saucepan in cold water and beat till cold enough to make into small balls. Take 1/2 cake of baker's chocolate grated fine and set it in a bowl in a dish of boiling water to melt and when balls are cool enough roll in the chocolate with a fork. This amount will make 80. (VC)

Cocoanut Cones

1 lb of powdered sugar, 1/2 lb grated cocoanut, whites of 5 eggs whip the eggs adding the sugar gradually until it will stand alone. Then beat in the cocoanut, mould with hand into small cones set on a buttered paper in a pan, not let them touch each other, bake in a moderate oven. (VC)

Floating Islands

Take a large teacup of currants or raspberry jelly, two spoonfuls of rich sweet cream, the whites of three eggs, whip it to a froth with a whisk, have a deep dish ready with rich sweet milk, take up the froth with a spoon, drop in the milk, take care to keep them separate. (VVC)

Nothings

Work 2–3 eggs into as much flour as will make a very stiff paste; roll to the thickness of a dollar piece. Cut in small pieces and drop into boiling lard. When done lay them to drain. Put a spoonful of jelly [on each]. (VVC)

Snow Balls

Take 14 eggs, 1 quart milk, sugar and cinnamon to your taste, boil the milk with the sugar and cinnamon, having it boiling hot put as much flour in as to soften it so that the spoon will stand in it, stir it till it is cool enough that you can bear your hand in it, then put one egg in after another, then take it out in a tablespoon and put it in hot lard. (UC)

Apple Fritters

2 ladles of flour, 1 pint buttermilk, a little soda, 1 egg, cinnamon, and 4 apples beat fine, a little water, fry in a pan. Also a little salt and sugar. (UC)

Apple Fritters with Eggs

Beat 2 eggs light and stir them to a pint of milk and half pint water with flour enough to make a smooth batter (a pint bowl heaping full is enough), pare and core 6 large tart apples and chop them small, stir them into the batter and cook. (VVC)

Indian Fritters

Take 5 tablespoonsful of flour, boiling water, and 4 eggs, also a little salt. Put the flour in a basin, and pour over it sufficiently boiling water to make it into a stiff paste. Stir and beat it well to prevent it getting lumpy. Leave it a little time to cool, and then break into it the eggs (without beating them first). Stir all well together. Have ready some boiling lard or butter, drop a desert spoonful of butter in a time and fry the fritters to a light brown. (UC)

Jelly Fritter Batter

2 eggs, 1 pint milk, 1 pint bowl flour (or more), beat light—when baked in lard—put jelly on top of each. (VVC)

[Good Pudding]

Good pudding may be made without eggs, but they must have as little milk as will mix, and must boil 3 or 4 hours. A few spoonfuls of fresh small beer or one of yeast will answer instead of eggs. Snow is an excellent substitute for eggs in puddings or pancakes. Two large spoonfulls are equal to one egg. Eggs beaten separately are always better than when taken together. (VVC)

Cornstarch Pudding

1 quart of milk, 5 teaspoons of starch wet in milk, 3 eggs beat up and stirred in with the starch, and then into the milk, boiling, cook 3 minutes. (UC)

Cheap Pudding

1 pint rice and 12 apples of good size (sour), pare, core, and slice them, put the rice and apples in a bag leaving space enough for the rice to swell. [Boil until done.] Eat it with any sauce you like, sugar and butter are very nice. (UC)

To Make Plain Boiled Pudding

Take a pint of new milk, mix with it 6 eggs well beaten, 2 spoonfuls of flour, salt chopped fine may be added. (VVC)

A Plain Cheap Rice Pudding

Tie in a cloth 1/4 pound of rice, 1/2 pound of raisins stoned, and boil them 2 hours, but take care that you give the rice a good deal of room to swell. When it is done enough turn it in to a dish and bake one hour in oven with 2 [tablespoons] melted butter and sugar with a little nutmeg grated in it. (VVC)

Potato Pudding

Take 1 large potato, 3 eggs, 1 pint milk, 1 teacup of flour, 1 tablespoon of spirits, 1 teaspoon of cinnamon, 1 of spice, 1 of ginger, a little butter, sugar to your taste. (UC)

Hasty Pudding

Put some milk over the fire, with a bit of lemon peal or essence of lemon; let it boil; then having made a large cup of flour to a smooth paste, with a little cold milk, stir it, by degrees, into the boiling milk; let it boil, stirring it all the time until it is thick; then dip a bowl in cold water; pour the pudding in and let it cool a little before turning it out; eat with butter and sugar sauce. The juice of a lemon or a glass of wine is an improvement. (VVC)

Dandy Jack Pudding

4 eggs, 2 tablespoons of flour, 1 quart of sweet milk, 1 cup of sugar. Beat the sugar, flour, and yolks of the eggs together, with one cup of the milk. Scald the remainder of the milk and put the above into it. Flavor with lemon. Beat the whites of the eggs with a little sugar to a stiff froth and spread it on the top of the pudding and then brown it in the oven. (VC)

Indian Pudding

This is from a clipping. Although the collections contain hand-written recipes for this dish, they're illegible.

One pint of milk, three eggs, one tablespoonful of molasses, one tablespoonful of butter, one half cup of flour, one tablespoonful of baking powder, one tablespoonful of mixed spice, Indian meal to make a batter. Scald the milk, and when boiling hot stir in Indian meal till the spoon moves stiffly. When cold add the eggs well beaten, and all the other ingredients. Bake in a buttered dish two hours, in a very slow oven. Serve with hot, sweet sauce. (VVC)

Apple Pudding

Select juicy apples that are a little tart. Pare, core, and cut them in small pieces, when you have 3 pints put them to boil. Let them stew till entirely done, take them off the stove, mash them well, add a lump of butter the size of a small egg, sugar to taste, and a very little cinnamon. When cold beat in 3 eggs. Butter the sides and bottom of a deep baking dish. Stir in bread crumbs until the bottom is covered an inch thick then about 1/2 the depth of the stewed apples a thin layer of crumbs the rest of the apples and another thick layer of crumbs. Set it in oven to bake which is quick, will take 1/2 an hour. Just before baking out sift white sugar over the top, put it in the hottest part a minute or two. Either cut cold with cream or hot sauce. (VVC)

Boiled Apple Pudding with Eggs

Batter of 2 eggs, 1 1/2 pt milk, with a pint bowl of flour, beat smooth and light; add 6 tender tart apples/prepared, and stir in the batter, tie in the pudding [bag] and boil 2 hours and serve with sauce. (VVC)

Feather Pudding

Cream together one scant cupful of sugar with two tablespoonfuls of butter, add one well beaten egg, one cupful of sweet milk, two cupfuls of flour mixed and sifted with three teaspoonfuls of baking powder, and a pinch of salt. Put two tablespoonfuls of any kind of berries, or cherries if preferred, either fresh or canned, in well-buttered cups, cover with the batter. Steam for one hour. Serve with sugar and cream or butter sauce. (VVC)

Cocoanut Pudding

To 1 1/2 pints of grated cocoanut add 1 pint of new milk, 2 cups of sweet and 4 eggs the yolks and white beaten separately, 2 teaspoonsful of melted butter, 2 crackers rolled fine, sweeten to taste. (VVC)

[Everyday Cocoanut Pudding]

A very nice plain mixture for cocoanut pudding suitable for everyday life is made by making a [paste] of 1 quart milk and 4 tablespoons of cornstarch, while hot melt a small piece of butter in it, let it cool and add the yolks, [ ] to taste and about a teacupful of grated cocoanut then the beaten whites. Both this and the preceding require the fire dishes lined with puff paste the mixture poured in bake in rather a quick oven 3/4 of an hour. (VVC)

Cocoanut and Sweet Potato Pudding

Grate whichever you intend to take, work 1 lb fine white sugar into 6 ounces butter, beat 6 eggs light, then add them to the sugar and butter, sprinkle the cocoanut (or sweet potato) gradually in, stir well, add a wine glass brandy or wine with nutmeg—line a deep dish with pie crust, put in the pudding, set in a quick oven— roll same paste thin; when the pudding has been in the oven 1/2 an hour, take it out; make a wreath of the leaves, put it on the edge and return to the oven for 15 minutes. (VVC)

Pumpkin Pudding

1 1/2 pound stewed pumpkin, 3 eggs, 1/4 pound butter [half?] a pint of cream, 1/2 pound sugar, 1/2 glass of rose water, mace, cinnamon. (VVC)

Plum Pudding

A very nice one for everyday use can be made by breaking into small pieces a stale loaf of baked bread, letting it soak in milk until it has absorbed all it will, draining it off thoroughly, and working out all the milk you can with a spoon. If you have any beef suet, add a little but it will do nicely without. Then stir in 1/2 teaspoonful of molasses, 1/2 pound brown sugar, the same quantity of stone raisins, 1/4 lb of currants rolled in flour, and a few pieces of citron if you have it. Boil in either a mould or pudding bag the same time you would an ordinary plum pudding the same size. Eat with sauce. (VVC)

German Pudding

"Good but troublesome."

Stir 1/2 pint sifted flour into 1 pint boiling milk, a little salt and then 1 ounce melted butter, put this over a moderate fire and stir till it thickens. Take it off, but stir yet. When quite smooth put on the stove again adding a little at a time 2 ounces sugar, more, 1 more of melted butter, more salt, yolks of 4 eggs. Keep stirring over fire till frothy, add the beaten whites, then pour into a buttered mould [and] with fine [sifted?] flour, [put] it in double boiler. In 3/4 of an hour, turn out and serve with hard or soft sauce. (VVC)

German Chocolate Pudding

2 ounces fine flour, 2 ounces butter, 1/4 pound fine [ ] sugar, yolks of 3 and white of 2 eggs, 1/4 pound fine grated chocolate. [Add] gradually into a pint of milk over a gentle fire till smooth and tolerably stiff; if too thick add a little milk, let it boil well. Stir it after till it cools, add 2 ounces butter (again) yolks of 6 more eggs, beat the whites to a froth, add them just before you put the mixture in a buttered dish, not more than 3/4 full. Powder the top with sugar, bake in a moderate oven. It should rise 3 or 4 inches above the dish, be of a yellow brown at the top. (VVC)

Chocolate Pudding

1 quart milk
1/2 cup chocolate grated
3 tablespoons cornstarch
4 tablespoons sugar
Yolk of 2 eggs

Heat slowly until the milk is boiling and the chocolate dissolved. When cool spread on the the top the whites beaten with sugar. Brown in the oven. (VVC)

Charlotte de' Russe

From Mrs. L.E. Meinung

Like 1 ounce of gelatin, 4 eggs, 1/2 pound of loaf sugar, 3 pints of cream. Vanilla to the taste. Part the gelatin into one pint of sweet milk several hours before using, then put on the fire and stir well until dissolved—don't let it boil. Beat the eggs separately, the whites smooth, not stiff. Put the gelatin milk warm into the yolks, next the sugar, then the whites, and lastly the whips from the cream and vanilla. (VVC)

Snow Cream

Put to a quart of cream the whites of 3 eggs, well beaten, 4 spoonfuls of sweet wine, sugar to your taste, and a bit of lemon peel; whip to a froth, remove the peel, and serve in a dish. (VVC)

Custard

1 pt sweet milk, a little lemon peel, and a stick of cinnamon. Boil briskly, meanwhile beat thoroughly the yolks of 3 eggs in a pint of sweet cream. As soon as the flavor of the spice is perceptible in the milk, pour it into the cream, stirring well and sweeten to your taste. Simmer the custard till it is of the desired thickness, but do not permit it to boil. Pour into cups, grate nutmeg, add the whites (beaten) with jelly if [desired]. (VVC)

Custard Without Eggs

One quart of new milk, 4 tablespoonfulls of flour, 2 spoonfulls sugar, season it with nutmeg and cinnamon. Add a little salt. Set the milk over the fire, when it boils pour on the flour, which should be previously stirred up in a little cold milk. When it is thoroughly scalded add the sugar, spice, and salt, and bake it either in crust or cups. (VVC)

To Make Egg Cheese [Custard]

So you take 8 eggs (more or less according to whether your molding-form is large or small). Beat them into a froth in a bowl. Add a half quart of sweet milk and let it run through a cloth or fine sieve. Then put it in a pot with a whole stick of cinnamon and also some lemon or coriander peel. Then put a large kettle with water on the fire and put the pot in it. Then stir it (you have to use a spoon). When it is thick enough you put it in the form and let it set up and become cold. When you serve it up you put sweet cream over it, and if you want, you can also sprinkle some ground cinnamon on the cheese. (WC)

Boiled Custard

One cup of milk, 1 egg, 1 tablespoon full of sugar. Soft ginger cake, 6 cups flour, 3 cups molasses, 1 of cream, 1 of butter, 1 tablespoon of ginger, 1/2 a spoonful of soda. (UC)

Buttermilk Custard

3 eggs, 2 cups sugar, 1/2 cup butter, 1 pint buttermilk, 3 heaping spoonsful flour, flavor with essence lemon. This [makes] quantity of 3 pies. (UC)

Iris Hege's Icecream

1 pt milk, 2 yolks eggs, 6 oz sugar, 1 tablespoon cornstarch. Scald all until it thickens. When cool add 1 pint whipped cream, after turning a little fast, add the whites of 2 eggs beaten stiff. Sweeten before and flavor. (VVC)

Recipe for Icecream

To 1 quart of milk put 2 eggs and 1/2 teacup sugar. Beat the yolks thoroughly, add them and the sugar to the milk and strain. Then froth the whites and add to the same. One pint of cream to 2 quarts of milk is a good mixture. Allow no sugar nor eggs for the first of cream. Flavor to taste. Boiling all the milk before adding eggs and sugar, with a tablespoon of corn starch makes freezing easier, but I think it better without boiling and the cornstarch. (VVC)

Lemon Ice Cream

For lemon ice cream have ready 2 quarts of very rich milk and take out 1 pint. Stir gradually into the pint 1/2 pound white sugar with a few drops oils of lemon. Afterwards, beat it gradually and hard into the remaining 3 pints cover it and let it stand in water about 1 hour. In damp weather it requires a longer time to freeze. You can add for each quart of milk [2?] tablespoonsful arrowroot rubbed smooth in a little cold milk. (VVC)

10

PRESERVES & PICKLES

I N THE EIGHTEENTH century when Salem was established, the domestic ritual of "putting up" fruits and vegetables (and drying meat) was a necessity. Storing up the summer surpluses for winter eating was essential to ensure the possibility that a family would have enough food and a better variety of items.

In those days, a household served as a home food factory because a food "industry" did not yet exist. Commercial canning wasn't widely accessed until the later 1800s; therefore, processing foods on a daily basis and putting up foods for later use consumed a large portion of time. The Mason jar, perfected in 1859, helped hasten canning; home canning became prevalent with the development of the pressure cooker in 1874.[14]

To Keep Preserves

Apply the white of an egg, with a suitable brush, to a single thickness of white tissue paper, with which cover the jars, overlapping the edges an inch or two. When dry, the whole will become as tight as a drum. (VVC)

Currant Jelly

1 lb. sugar to 1 pint juice—take off scum while boiling. (VVC)

Salem Diary, Dec. 19, 1788

"We had the first snow, but only a small one which melted the same day. There is a hard wind from the northwest, and it has grown so cold that we feel it was not equalled last winter, as severe as that was. Unfortunately the only thermometer in town, privately owned, has been broken. The effect of the cold has been felt more than last winter, because the vegetables in the cellars and those buried in the ground have been frozen, though there may have been contributory circumstances."[15]

To Make Peach Preserves

Take 6 pounds of yellow pared peaches nicely cut from the stone, add 5 lbs crushed sugar, let them stand overnight, then boil over a slow fire, about 20 minutes, then take the peaches out, then boil the syrup down till it is nearly done, then put the peaches in again and boil till done (put in a few roots of ginger or when you begin to boil them, it improves the flavor). (UC)

Canning Peaches

To fill 6 half gallon cans take 3 pecks of peaches, two pounds crushed sugar. Pare and cut in half, then put the peaches and sugar together and water enough to start them to boil, say half way up the peaches. Boil till you can stick a fork through easily, then put them in the cans as hot as possible or as soon as you can after they are done, and have them sodered up immediately and keep them in a cool, dry place. (UC)

Tomato Honey

To each pound of tomatoes allow the grated peel of a lemon and six fresh peach leaves. Boil them slowly till they are all to pieces, then squeeze them through a bag. To each pound of liquid allow a pound of sugar and the juice of one lemon. Boil them together half an hour or till they become a thick jelly. Then put it into glasses and lay double tissue paper over the top. It will scarcely be distinguished from real honey. (VVC)

On Preserving Butter

From a newspaper clipping dated 1844.

...There are many things required to ensure good butter. The butter itself must be well made—that is, worked enough, and not too much, and salted with rock salt. This being well done, and the buttermilk all expelled, the butter may be packed in good white oak (well seasoned) casks, well filled....In hot climates, it is best to have small casks—say from 25 to 30 pounds; so that too much need not be exposed while using. Then put these small casks into a hogshead and fill up the same with strong pickle that will bear an egg, and the butter may be shipped from the West Indies or Europe, and kept perfectly sweet....To keep butter in ice-houses, when it remains frozen, will answer, if the butter is to be continued in the same temperature; but if it is exposed to warm weather, after being taken from the ice, it will not keep as long as if it had not been exposed to so cold a temperature. (VVC)

To Make Apple Sauce or Apple Butter

Take new cider from the press, boil it down in a brass or belmetal kettle till the skum has done rising, or till it is boiled one third away; pare your apples, let them be neither sweet nor sour, but tender; put them in the cider, boil it till it is all mixed and thick, be careful not to let it burn; put it up in a stone pot for use; this makes very good tarts, adding a little sugar, rose water, cinnamon, or orange peel. (VVC)

Apple Butter

5 gallons sweet cider (boil the same day it is pressed), boil it down to half, then strain through a cloth and then put in 1 peck of pared apples, then boil till the apples are soft, then press them through a colender after which you put them back into the cider again, with four pounds of sugar, and boil until it is thick enough to keep. (UC)

For Canning or Drying Beef Tongues

Lay in salt overnight or day and night. To 50 lbs beef take 3 gallons water, 3 quarts salt, 3 1/4 lbs sugar, 2 oz salt petre, some red pepper. Let the beef be in a week or so or longer if the pieces are thick or for only a few longer. Take 2 quarts water, 2 pints salt, 1 tablespoon of salt petre, and a handful of sugar; you need not boil the brine, only stir it well. (UC)

Meat Pickle

To one gallon of water take one and one half pounds of salt, one half pounds of sugar, one half ounce of saltpetre, one half ounce of potash. (VC)

Chow Chow

1 gallon green tomatoes, 1 gallon of cabbage (after it is cut fine), 4 pods of green peppers, chop all well together. Put in salt overnight then squeeze out and put in a jar with the spices and sugar then pour vinegar to cover. Set away. Use the vinegar cold. Two cups of sugar, 1 cup of mixed mustard seed, 1 tablespoon of ground cloves, 1 of all-spice, 2 of cinnamon. Mix all together and pack in a jar. (UC)

[Vogler] Chow Chow

One peck of green tomatoes, one half peck of onions, two large
cabbages, 1 tablespoon ground cloves, 1 tablespoon ground spice,
1 quart of green pepper, chop fine, strew thickly with salt, let
stand over night, cook soft and cover with good vinegar. Horse
radish improves it. Celery seed and white mustard seed. (VC)

[Tips for Good] Pickles

Kettles of black tin are the best for pickling. Brass could be used
but thoroughly cleansed and no vinegar allowed to cool in them.
Boil alum and salt in the vinegar, 1/2 a teacup of salt and a tablespoonful of alum to a gallon vinegar. Put up in stone or wood. All
pickles should be stirred up occasionally. When scum arises the
vinegar ought to scald and when it becomes weak from use, fresh
vinegar should be substituted. Good but not the sharpest vinegar
should be used for pickles. The jars should always be full enough
of vinegar to cover the pickles. The vinegar should only boil 5–6
minutes. The best cucumbers are the small green of quick growth.
Turn boiling water on them as soon as pickles [ ] them remain 5
hours and then in cold vinegar with alum and slat. When you
have done collecting the cucumbers for pickling, turn the vinegar
from the cucumbers, scald and skim it till [ ] thin, put in the
pickles let them scald without boiling, for a few minutes then turn
them while hot into the vessel you intend to keep them in. A few
peppercorns improve the taste of the cucumbers. (VVC)

Sweet Pickles (Mrs. Mickey)

To 3 pounds fruit or rind, 1 pint vinegar, 1 lb sugar, cut melon or
fruit in slices and put vinegar sugar and spices together and make
boiling hot and pour over melon. Scald them every other morning
for two weeks. (UC)

Watermelon Pickle

Soak in strong salt water 3 days and nights. Keep in the sun and
stir around occasionally, then in fresh water 3 days and nights.
The 7th day put in alum water over night. Next morning, boil in
strong ginger water with cloves and whatever spice you wish,
then drain and weigh. Take 1 lb. sugar to 1 lb. rind and to every
2 lbs sugar 1 cup warm water, boil in this till clear and tender,
then take out, add vinegar to taste, let it boil, return the rind and
boil 15 minutes. (VC)

Watermelon Sweet Pickle

Pare off the outer rind and cut in pieces. Lay in cold vinegar or salt water overnight. Then take as much fresh vinegar as will cover the rind. To 1 quart of vinegar take half a pound sugar (if the vinegar is very <u>strong</u> it is better to take 1 lb of sugar). Add cloves, mace, cinnamon bark to the taste; simmer the rind a short time, then skim out and boil down the syrup well. The syrup will require boiling several times... (UC)

Watermelon Preserved

A thick rind is preferred; pare off the outer green and use the most solid part; to 1 lb of rind take 1 lb of sugar. Soak the rind in a good salt water for 24 hours; wash in fresh water and lay in alum water for 12 hours; then boil in clear water 5 minutes. Dissolve the sugar with a little water and when boiling lay in the rind and boil until it looks clear. Take it out to cool and boil down the syrup until it is thick. Flavor with ginger or cloves. (UC)

Watermelon Rind Pickle

For 10 pounds put the pieces cut as you like into your kettle well covered with water. Let them boil a few minutes, then lay on dishes to drain and cool. Pour away all the water, put the rind into the kettle when cool. Cover with vinegar and three pounds of sugar, seasoned to taste with mace, cloves, and all spice, ginger. Let it boil till tender. For three or four mornings successively pour off the vinegar, bring it to boiling and pour over the pickle. (VC)

Pickle Peaches

To three pounds of fruit peeled or not, stones taken out or not, take 1 lb of sugar, 1 pint of vinegar with spices cinnamon, cloves, ginger, and all spice to your taste. The syrup to be poured on boiling hot, and to be repeated 8 or 9 times [for] a week. (VC)

Green Tomato Pickle

Into a quart of good sharp vinegar put 1 tablespoonful each of ground cinnamon, cloves, allspice, and grated nutmeg, 1 teaspoon each of black and white pepper, 1 lb of brown sugar. Put this in a brass kettle over a moderately quick fire and when it boils have ready about 2 quarts of green and ripe tomatoes, and put them in. Let them boil until tender, dip them out into a jar and pour the hot vinegar over them. (VC)

Green Tomatoes Pickle

Slice them fine, and let them stand overnight. Mix with it horse radish, onions, and green pepper cut fine, also salt. In the morning, press all the salt water out, press them in a jar, pour over them cold strong vinegar with a little sugar. (VC)

Pickled Onions

Take a regular sized onion. Pare and boil in salt water till they can be easily pierced with a fork then put them into a jar then put your cloves and sugar into your vinegar and boil 4 or 5 minutes then pour it over your onions and put them away for use. (UC)

Chopped Green Tomato Pickle

1 gallon tomatoes chopped fine, 1 quart chopped onions, put in jar with salt sprinkled on them and let them lay over night, in the morning take them out of the salt and squeeze the water out of them. Vinegar enough to cover the tomatoes, 1/2 box of mustard, teaspoonful of cayenne pepper, tablespoonful of cinnamon, same of mace and black pepper and a few cloves, 1/2 pound of sugar. Put in a kettle with all the ingredients and boil until tender. (UC)

Memor. of Salem Congregation, 1843

"[God] has in general cared for us and ours as a father and bestowed upon us fruitful times and a blessed harvest while the field and garden fruits and those of the trees throve and with the still not improved depression of circumstances in business circles, still no one of us had to suffer need." [16]

"The church relinquished economic control
of Old Salem in the mid-nineteenth century.
But its spiritual influence remains strong,
and the rich culture it shaped endures." [17]

GLOSSARY

American reflector: A spitted oven rack used to roast meat, fowl, fish, or fruit on the fire.

arrowroot: A light starch used in desserts made from the root-stock of a tropical, perennial plant and used as a thickener in cooking; the plant also had medicinal value as its tubers were used to draw poison from wounds.

avoirdupois weight: A system of weights and measures based on a pound containing 16 ounces or 7,000 grains and equal to 453.59 grams.

baking powder: Introduced in 1856, this modern-day convenience combined saleratus (baking soda) and cream of tartar.

beef suet: The hard fatty tissues around the kidneys of cattle and sheep and used in cooking and for making tallow.

belmetal/bell-mettle: Variant spellings of bellmetal, a bronze made of four parts of copper to one of tin; it was purported to be superior in certain respects to plain copper (it was less likely to affect flavor) or tinned copper (it was more durable).

bruise: To crush or pound into pieces.

Claret: A dry red wine.

citron: A thorny shrub or small tree widely cultivated for its large lemonlike fruits that have a thick warty rind.

citron melon: A large, lemon-like fruit with a thick rind from the citron shrub/tree; its rind is often candied for use in cakes, confections, and puddings, and aromatic oils are extracted from the rind.

Damask rose: A rose (Rosa damascena) native to Asia; it has fragrant red or pink flowers and is used as a source of fragrant essential oil or perfume.

Dutch oven: A heavy three-legged (cast iron) pot or kettle used for slow cooking; a metal utensil open on one side, with shelves, used with an open fire for baking or roasting food; a wall oven in which food is baked utilizing its preheated brick walls.

gill: Liquid measure equalling 1/4 pint.

gravy: Referred to for broth or stock.

gum arabic: A gum from acacia that was used in medicine, candy, and ink.

hartshorn: Deer antlers, which were shaved and provided an equivalent to modern-day gelatin.

hogshead: A liquid measure equal to large cask with a capacity of usually 63–140 gallons.

hops: The main ingredient in yeast, but sometimes hard to get in the South. The herb "life everlasting" and artichoke leaves could be used in place of hops.

Indian meal: An old-fashioned name for corn meal.

lard: The fat of a hog that was used as a major oil in cooking, through the mid-1900s, especially in the South, until the invention of Crisco and other replacements.

life everlasting: A herbaceous biennial growing from 1–3 feet tall with green leaves and clusters of small, white flower heads. It was one of the most highly regarded remedies for sale in local markets of the Southern United States through the early 1900s. It was often used in several ways: as an astringent tea, a bitter herbal cold medicine, and the leaves and blossoms chewed. (see endnote #4)

lights: An animal's lungs; called "lights" because of the lightness in weight.

loaf sugar: A cone-shaped mass of concentrated sugar.

lunar caustic: Sticks of silver nitrate used to burn or sear items.

milk warm: Of a luke warm temperature.

orange water: Made by steeping or distilling orange flower petals in water. Used as a flavoring through the 18th century, but less common than rose water; again coming into use, flower water is expensive. Use sparingly as you would flavorings and herbs.

pearl ash: An impure form of potassium carbonate.

pitch: A resin derived from the sap of various coniferous trees, including the North American pine, which yields a resin used as turpentine.

pot ash/potash: Any of a variety of potassium compounds; also called caustic potash or lye; also "pot ashes," from the Dutch "potaschen" (obtained by leaching wood ashes and evaporating the leach in a pot).

puncheon: A cask with a capacity of from 72 to 120 gallons; the amount of liquid contained in a puncheon.

rabbit grease: When cooking a rabbit, the skim that forms on top.

rose water/rosewater: Made by steeping or distilling fresh petals in water. Used as a flavoring through the 18th century; again coming into use, flower water is expensive. Use sparingly as you would flavorings and herbs.

rub: Sometimes used in place of the word "mix."

sal ammoniac: Also known as ammonium chloride, this was used as a soldering flux and an expectorant.

saleratus: A precursor to baking power, this form of baking soda was introduced around 1840, and required adding cream of tartar to work; it was used to leaven products where it was undesirable to use yeast. A substitute for saleratus was lye or potash, which acted as a leavening agent. (In 1873, two druggists from Fort Wayne, Indiana, Thomas Biddle and James Hoagland, came up with the formula of baking soda and cream of tartar that was later marketed as Royal Baking Powder.)

saltpetre/salt petre: Variant spellings of salt peter, which was potassium nitrate—a common food preservative in the eighteenth-century.

slaked lime: Another term for calcium hydroxide, which is a soft white powder used in making such items as calcium salts.

syllabub: A beverage made of sweetened milk or cream curdled with wine or spirits; can also refer to a cold dessert made with cream, sometimes thickened with gelatin, and mixed with wine, spirits, or fruit juice.

tallow: Made from one of a number of vegetable or animal fats and used in making candles and soap.

NOTES

────────────── (FRONT MATTER) ──────────────
1. Adelaide L. Fries, MA, ed., *Records of the Moravians in North Carolina Volume I (1752–1771)*. (Raleigh: State Department of Archives and History, 1922), 79.
2. Adelaide L. Fries, MA, ed., *Records of the Moravians in North Carolina Volume II (1752–1775)*. (Raleigh: State Department of Archives and History, rep. 1968), 558.

────────────── SECTION 1 ──────────────
3. Adelaide L. Fries, MA, ed., *Records of the Moravians in North Carolina Volume IV (1780–1783)*. (Raleigh: State Department of Archives and History), 1579.

────────────── SECTION 2 ──────────────
4. Kirkland, J., H.F. Mathews, C.W. Sullivan III, and K. Baldwin, eds. *Herbal and Magic Medicine: Traditional Healing Today*.(Durham, North Carolina, and London: Duke University Press, 1992).
5. Adelaide L. Fries, MA, ed., *Records of the Moravians in North Carolina Volume II (1752–1775)*. (Raleigh: State Department of Archives and History, rep. 1968), 564–565.

────────────── SECTION 4 ──────────────
6. Adelaide L. Fries, MA, ed., *Records of the Moravians in North Carolina Volume V (1784–1792)*. (Raleigh: State Department of Archives and History), 2281.
7. Adelaide L. Fries, MA, Litt. D. and Douglas LeTell Rights, A.B., B.D., STB, DD, eds. *Records of the Moravians in North Carolina Volume VIII (1823–1837)*.(Raleigh: State Department of Archives and History, 1954), 4171.

────────────── SECTION 5 ──────────────
8. Adelaide L. Fries, MA, ed., *Records of the Moravians in North Carolina Volume II (1752–1775)*. (Raleigh: State Department of Archives and History, rep. 1968), 563, 565, 573–576.

────────────── SECTION 7 ──────────────
9. Adelaide L. Fries, MA, ed., *Records of the Moravians in North Carolina Volume V (1784–1792)*. (Raleigh: State Department of Archives and History), 2268.

10. Adelaide L. Fries, MA, ed., *Records of the Moravians in North Carolina Volume IV (1780–1783).* (Raleigh: State Department of Archives and History), 1752.

——————————— SECTION 8 ———————————

11. Adelaide L. Fries, MA, ed., *Records of the Moravians in North Carolina Volume VII (1809–1822).* (Raleigh: State Department of Archives and History, 1947), 3339.

——————————— SECTION 9 ———————————

12. Beth Tartan, *North Carolina & Old Salem Cookery.* (Chapel Hill, NC: University of North Carolina Press, 1992), 69.

13. _____. "The Moravian Star," *The Moravian*, (December 2000), 14.

——————————— SECTION 10 ———————————

14. Lily May and John Spaulding. *Civil War Recipes: Receipts from the Pages of Godey's Lady's Book.* (Lexington, KY: The University Press of Kentucky, 1999), 16.

15. Adelaide L. Fries, MA, ed., *Records of the Moravians in North Carolina Volume V (1784–1792).* (Raleigh: State Department of Archives and History), 2226.

16. Minnie J. Smith, ed., *Records of the Moravians in North Carolina Volume IX (1838–1847).* (Raleigh: State Department of Archives and History, 1964), 4713.

17. Maureen Palmedo, *Visiting Our Past: America's Historylands.* (Washington, DC: National Geographic Society), 127.

THE FOLLOWING WERE EXCELLENT REFERENCES:

* Burroughs, Frances M. "The Confederate Receipt Book: A Study in Food Substitution in the American Civil War." *South Carolina Historical and Genealogical Magazine* 93 (Jan. 1992): 31–50.

* Camp, Charles. American Foodways: What, When, Why, and How We Eat in America, Little Rock: August House, Inc. 1989.

* Porcher, Frances P. *Resources of the Southern Fields and Forests.* Charleston, SC: Evans & Cogswell, 1863.

* Spaulding, Lily May and John. *Civil War Recipes: Receipts from the Pages of Godey's Lady's Book.* Lexington, KY: The University Press of Kentucky, 1999.

SELECTED BIBLIOGRAPHY

FOR FURTHER READING

A SURPRISINGLY VAST wealth of books exists on our country's earlier years of cooking and housekeeping. For those individuals interested in exploring more fully this subject, the following abbreviated list of titles is offered. Some books will only be found in private libraries (start searching your attic) or in professional collections. Many others not listed are also available. The following has been narrowed according to those that relate more completely to Southern cooking/housekeeping or "American" cookery and homekeeping at large.

Beecher, Catharine. *Miss Beecher's Domestic Receipt Book.* New York: Harper & Brothers, 1849.

Beecher, Catharine, and Stowe, Harriet Beecher. *The New Housekeeper's Manual: Embracing a New Revised Edition of the American Woman's Home.* New York: J.B. Ford and Co., 1873.

Blot, Pierre. *Hand-Book of Practical Cookery.* 1867. Reprint, New York: Amo Press, 1973.

Chadwick, Mrs. J. *Home Cookery.* 1852. Reprint, Birmingham, AL: Oxmoor House, 1984.

Child, Lydia Maria. *The American Frugal Housewife.* 1832. Reprint, Bedford, MA: Applewood Books, n.d.

[Crowen, Mrs. T.J.]. *The American Lady's System of Cookery.* New York: Derby and Miller, 1852.

Crump, Nancy Carter. *Hearthside Cooking.* McLean, Virginia: EPM Publications, Inc., 1986.

Farrington, Doris. *Fireside Cooks & Black Kettle Recipes.* Indianapolis: Bobbs-Merrill Company, 1976.

Fisher, Abby. *What Mrs. Fisher Knows about Old Southern Cooking.* 1881. Reprint. Bedford, MA: Applewood Books, 1995.

Hale, Mrs. Sarah Hosepha. *The Good Housekeeper.* 1841. Reprint, Mineola, NY: Dover Publications, 1996.

Harland, Marion. *Common Sense in the Household, A Manual of Practical Housewifery.* New York: Charles Scribner's Sons, 1881.

Harrison, Molly. *The Kitchen in History.* New York: Charles Scribner's Sons, 1972.

Hess, Karen, ed. *Martha Washington's Booke of Cookery and Booke of Sweetmeats.* N.d. Reprint with extensive commentary, New York: Columbia University Press, 1981.

Hill, Annabella P. *Mrs. Hill's Southern Practical Cookery and Receipt Book.* 1872. Reprint, Columbia, SC: University of South Carolina Press, 1995.

Lantz, Louise K. *Old American Kitchenware: 1725–1925.* Camden, New York: Thomas Nelson Inc.; Hanover, Pennsylvania: Everybody's Press, 1970.

Leslie, Eliza. *Directions for Cookery.* 1837. Reprint of 1848 edition, New York: Arno Press, 1973.

Lowenstein, Eleanor. *Bibliography of American Cookery Books, 1742–1860.* Worcester, MA: American Antiquarian Society, 1972.

Plante, Ellen M. *The American Kitchen, 1700 to the Present.* New York: Facts on File, 1995.

Porter, Mrs. M.F. *Mrs. Porter's New Southern Cookery Book.* 1871. Reprint, New York: Arno Press, 1973.

Putnam, Mrs. (Elizabeth H.). *Mrs. Putnam's Receipt Book and Young Housekeeper's Assistant.* New York: Sheldon and Co., 1867.

Rutledge, Sarah. *The Carolina Housewife.* 1847. Reprint, Columbia, SC: University of South Carolina Press, 1979.

Shute, Miss T.S. *The American Housewife Cook Book.* Philadelphia: George T. Lewis and Menzies Company, 1880.

Simmons, Amelia. *American Cookery.* 1796. Reprint, Bedford, MA: Applewood Books, 1996.

Strasser, Susan. *Never Done: A History of American Housework.* New York: Pantheon, 1982.

Tartan, Beth. *Noth Carolina & Old Salem Cookery.* Chapel Hill, NC: University of North Carolina Press, 1992.

Thorton, P. *The Southern Gardener and Receipt Book.* Newark, New Jersey: A.L. Dennis, publisher, 1845.

[Webster, Mrs. A.L.] *The Improved Housewife.* 1845. Reprint, New York: Amo Press, 1973.

RESOURCE LIST

—— INGREDIENTS AND ITEMS FOR RECREATING RECIPES ——

* Heirloom seeds and plants:
    Landis Valley Museum Heirloom Seed Project
    2451 Kissel Hill Road, Lancaster, PA 17601-4899
    (717)569-0401 or fax: (717)560-2147

* Old-fashioned chemicals (for example, they carry ammonium carbonate, also known as "hartshorn," an old-fashioned and hard-to-find ingredient for making cookies crisp):
    Tri-EssSciences
    1020 W. Chestnut Street, Burbank, California 91506
    (800)274-6910 or (818)848-7838
    www.Tri-EssSciences.com

* Old-fashioned merchandise:
    Lehman's Non-Electric
    One Lehman Circle, P.O. Box 321, Kidron, OH 44636
    (888)438-5346 or (330)857-5757
    www.Lehmans.com

* Orange flower water and other old-fashioned ingredients:
    Chef Shop
    PO Box 3488, Seattle, WA 98114-3488
    (877)337-2491 or (206)286-9988
    http://store.yahoo.com/chefshop/orflowwat.html

* Replicas of historic cookie molds:
    House on the Hill
    650 West Grand Ave., Unit 100, Elmhurst, IL 60126
    (630)279-4455
    www.houseonthehill.net

* Reproduction tinware:
    Michael Felk, tinsmith
    153 N. Lee Avenue, Yadkinville, NC 27055
    (336)679-7179

* Reproductions of 17th–18th century glassware:
    P&B Glassworks
    5612 Mooretown Road, Unit C, Williamsburg, VA 23188
    (757)564-8436

* Reproductions of 17th–19th stoneware:
    Westmoore Pottery
    4622 Busbee Road, Seagrove, NC 27341
    (910)464-3700
    www.westmoorepottery.com

* Spices:
    Adriana's Caravan
    78 Grand Central Terminal, New York, NY 10017
    (800)316-0820 or (212)972-8804
    www.adrianascaravan.com

* Various goods for historical cookery and living:
    Francesco Sirene, Spicer
    Box 1051, Peachland, B.C., Canada V0H 1X0
    www.silk.net/sirene/

────────────────── LIBRARIES ──────────────────

* Indiana University, Lilly Library Collections
    1200 E. Seventh Street, Indiana University
    Bloomington, IN 47405-5500
    (812)855-2452
    www.indiana.edu/~liblilly/text/lillyhome.html

* Johnson & Wales University, Culinary Archives & Museum
    315 Harborside Boulevard, Providence, RI 02905
    www.culinary.org

* University of Houston, Hospitality Industry Archives
    229 C. N. Hilton Hotel and College, Houston, TX 77204-3028
    (713)743-2470
    www.hrm.uh.edu

* Vorhoff Library, Newcomb College Center for Research on Women
    Tulane University, New Orleans, LA 70118
    (504)865-5762
    www.voyager.tcs.tulane.edu/

────────────────── OTHER RESOURCES ──────────────────

* A history of Salem, including a wonderful map:
    www.1766salem.org/history2.htm

* K–12 teacher resources for food history lessons;
    "The Food Timeline" provides food beginnings and historic recipes;
    "Culinary History Timeline" gives customs, menus, and manners:
    www.gti.net/mocolib1/kid/food2.html

* Southern Foodways Alliance, an affiliated institute of the Center for
    the Study of Southern Culture. The mission of the SFA is to celebrate,
    preserve, promote, and nurture the traditional and developing diverse
    food cultures of the American South:
    www.southernfoodways.com

IF YOU'D LIKE TO LEARN MORE about the Moravians, visit the Moravian
Archives; the North Carolina settlements of Old Salem (est. 1766),
Bethabara (est. 1753), Bethania (est. 1756); or attend a regular or special
service at one of the many Moravian churches. To buy books about the
Moravians in North Carolina, the Moravian Archives and the Moravian
Book & Gift Shop in Old Salem offer various titles.

INDEX

ACKNOWLEDGEMENTS

THERE ARE MANY HANDS that went into kneading this collection into book form. The original hands that captured the recipes on pen and paper during their lives in early Salem must be thanked and remembered. Their collections are magnificent time capsules—from the ink (or pencil lead) they used and the kinds of paper to the beautiful language syntax. Often I would peek beneath the pasted-on receipts to read snippets of old composition books belonging to the young Van Vleck daughters. Their words were fascinating and captivating. Motivating, too, their words calling out to me from centuries past. While learning more about the original owners of the different recipe collections through reading the "Lebenslauf" (memoir) of some of the authors, I wished that I could be privy to more complete details of their lives. Our foremothers were strong, intelligent, and talented.

The Moravian Archives and its skilled staff, particularly Dr. Daniel Crews and Richard Starbuck, were tremendously kind and helpful. Dr. Crews graciously translated some of the recipes that were written in German. Thank you to Bob Bennett and Nicole Blum also. The archives is the most agreeable of surroundings, making even the tediousness of deciphering aged writing exciting. Oh, the joy when a word was uncovered! *T'was there all along in plain sight.* And what a lovely contradiction to be entering those words on a laptop when my hands were fondling documents and thin wisps of paper with austere dates in the 1800s. Both the place and the people made it easy to step back in history: cream-colored books with brown stained pages to my right; farther, the trees and the equal markers of God's Acre. *All is right with the world in this place.*

Barbara Kuck, director of the Culinary Archives & Museum at Johnson & Wales University in Providence, Rhode Island, was also extremely kind for letting me camp out in the museum—during renovations—reading through some of the more than 8,000 cookbooks housed there. What a worthy trip North. And how validating also to read words of Salem, North Carolina, there. This was true, too, of my research trek to the Library of Congress in Washington, DC.

Closer home, I give appreciation to Barbara Ireland, librarian of Boonville Public Library, for happily tracking down scads of related cookbooks and works of history. Thanks also to Angie Walker, assistant librarian. Our public libraries hold a wealth of knowledge; our librarians hold the keys to unlock it. Barbara and Angie do an outstanding job, and our public librarians are overdue adequate support and thanks.

My parents are also owed thanks, not only for (Mother) serving as chief baker for some of the taste testings and (Daddy) giving a lifetime of Moravian knowledge and recollections to the included history, but also for lovingly weaving Moravian traditions into my life. They were also good resources for "old fashioned" terms and happenings. Moreover, my grandparents, aunts, and uncles have had strong roles in my three decades of education of all things Moravian.

Danke to my husband and best friend, Scott, for encouraging me to embark on this wonderful and wonderfully needed documentation. You made an amateur cook and beginning historian feel like a bona fide scholar.

And a heart-filled thanks to those various other individuals—family, friends, and strangers—who have helped throughout the process.

Emily-Sarah Lineback has edited numerous books and compiled several cookbooks, including serving as compiler and editor for *River Rations: Recipes & Recollections of Rural Living*, during her tenure at a book production firm. Her English degree from the University of North Carolina at Greensboro has enabled her a varied background including titles of newspaper copy editor, television news editor, magazine writer, and marketing director. She has led several marketing/writing workshops for state and national conferences.

A native North Carolinian, Lineback's childhood has been greatly influenced by her Moravian family (including her parents' encouragement to learn to play several instruments). She inherited a reverence for history and has had instilled in her a respect for God, church, tradition, family, and honest work. Her lineage can be traced back to some of the first Moravians in the state.

She has won several awards for her writing as well as for her community involvement (and, as her parents would like noted, for her abilities as a pianist). Readers can share their own Moravian experiences and memories by emailing Lineback via *carolinaavepress@yadtel.net.*